GCSE IN A WEEK

Author – Steven Croft

Use this day-by-day listing and the tabs on each page in the b...

D0230818

As part of your exam you may be asked to write imaginatively. This might involve writing your own story or the opening to a story. Stories are made up of various elements:

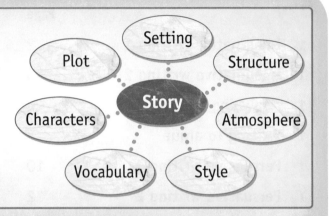

Planning your story

An effective story needs careful planning. There are two basic approaches:

Approach A: Create your main character or characters, then think of a storyline for them.

Approach B: Think of your storyline, then create the characters to fit it.

Once you have decided on your characters and plot you are ready to plan your story in more detail:

> It helps a lot if you base your story around something that you are familiar with.

1. the beginning – introducing the characters – setting the scene

2. development – key events – the build up

3. climax – the key moment/event

4. the ending – an effective conclusion

How to approach imaginative writing by using helpful strategies in planning; developing your characters, plot and setting; and getting started.

DAY 1

○ Beginning your story

Here are some approaches that different writers have used to make their openings effective.

A

Introduces character

Intriguing: raises reader's curiosity

It was a bright cold day in April, and **the clocks were striking thirteen. Winston Smith**, his chin nuzzled into his breast in an effort to **escape the vile wind**, slipped quickly through the glass doors of Victory Mansions, though not quickly enough to prevent a swirl of gritty dust form entering along with him.

Creates atmosphere

B

Captures attention

When a day that **you happen to know is Wednesday** starts off by sounding like Sunday, there is something seriously wrong somewhere.

Makes reader curious

C

Direct speech immediately captures reader's attention
Scene implied — reader works out what is going on

'There you are, Mrs Ebbs, hold the cup steady. Can you manage, dear? Whoops! That's it. Now sit up properly, you'll slip down in the bed again, sit up against your pillows.

D

Focuses on character

Emma Woodhouse, handsome, clever, and rich, with a comfortable home and happy disposition, seemed to unite some of the best blessings of existence; and had lived nearly twenty-one years in the world with very little to distress or vex her.

Gives details and background

When beginning your story you could:

- launch straight into the story by opening with direct speech
- focus on description of main character
- describe setting
- create a sense of atmosphere
- use a puzzling, unusual opening sentence or phrase

> **Whatever you do, interest your readers and capture their attention.**

IMAGINATIVE WRITING 2

Developing characters

Characters are a key element in your story. You must make your characters **convincing**. Writers use a number of techniques to make their characters convincing. Look at these two examples:

> **Example**
>
> **Extract A**
>
> Albert, the corporal, was a clean-shaven, shrewd-looking fellow of about forty. He seemed to think his one aim in life was to be full of fun and nonsense. In repose, his face looked a little withered, old. He was a very good pal to Joe, steady, decent and grave under all his 'mischief'; for his mischief was only his laborious way of skirting his own ennui.
>
> Joe was much younger than Albert – only twenty-three. He was a tallish, quiet youth, pleasant-looking. He was of a slightly better class than his corporal, more personable. Careful about his appearance, he shaved every day. 'I haven't got much of a face,' said Albert. 'If I was to shave every day like you, Joe, I should have none.'

Extract A

Here the writer:

- focuses on physical appearance and age
- indicates something about the attitudes of the characters
- uses some direct speech

Ways to give your reader a picture of your characters:	The examiner is looking for:
• what they look like	• original storyline
• what they say	• well-planned plot and setting
• how they say it	• convincing characters
• their attitudes and behaviour	• good writing style and vocabulary
• what others say about them	• effective structure
	• technical accuracy, e.g. spelling

○ Setting

If the setting is an important element in your story, then think carefully about how you describe it. Here is an example of a writer creating a setting:

Example

Extract B

July had been blown out like a candle by a biting wind that ushered in a leaden August sky. A sharp, stinging drizzle fell, billowing into opaque grey sheets when the wind caught it. Along the Bournemouth sea-front the beach-huts turned blank wooden faces towards a greeny-grey, froth-chained sea that leapt eagerly at the cement bulwark of the shore.

Extract B

Here the writer makes use of:

- well-chosen adjectives
- a simile
- personification
- details of the scene

ANALYSING ARGUMENTS

○ Making arguments work

Understanding how arguments can be presented to make the writer's point is important for two reasons:

1. In the exam, you might be given an example of an argument in some form and be asked to **analyse** it.

2. You might be asked to write your own argument. To do this to best effect you need to understand and use the techniques for constructing arguments that can influence the reader.

In the exam, arguments could be presented in a number of forms including newspaper and magazine articles, letters, pamphlets and newsletters.

Start by thinking about the **audience** and **purpose** of the argument you are given. Most arguments consist of a combination of **fact** and **opinion**. One of the first things you need to do when analysing an argument is to understand the different between the two.

● **Facts** are statements which are **true** (although some facts can be disputed).

● **Opinions** express a **point of view**, give a **judgement** on something or convey a personal **idea**.

There are a variety of features to help present an argument powerfully and effectively. Here are some of the key devices to watch out for:

● **Bias** – points made and facts stated are strongly influenced by opinion or prejudice so that one view is given, excluding alternative ideas.

● **Emotive language** – vocabulary and style are designed to appeal to particular emotions or provoke a particular feeling or response in the reader.

● **Rhetorical questions** – questions are used for effect rather than requiring an answer.

● **Repetition** – points or phrases are repeated for effect.

What the examiner is looking for:

● awareness of audience and purpose

● ability to distinguish between fact and opinion

● ability to identify bias

● awareness of emotive language and effects

● awareness of other language techniques

15 MINS

Example

Look at the following extract from an article on wind-powered energy.

Pollution, and in particular, 'greenhouse gas' emissions resulting from the burning of fossil fuels is an increasing problem to us all. Many believe that this is a major contributory factor in increased global warming and that we must do something about it before it is too late. Wind-generated power can provide the answer to this problem. Wind power can provide clean energy with no detrimental effect on the environment. The indisputable fact that wind-power is pollution free must therefore mean that this is the only sensible way forward. This is the way to prevent a catastrophe of cataclysmic proportions. This is the way to prevent the destruction of our environment. This is the way to ensure the survival of our planet.

Notice how this piece of writing makes use of:

- facts
- opinions
- bias
- repetition

Progress check

1 What is a fact?

2 What is an opinion?

3 What is emotive language designed to do?

4 'Have we had enough of this leadership? Do the people of this country want to carry on with this? No! they have had enough.'

What is the name for the highlighted feature?

DAY
1
2
3
4
5
6
7

Types of questions

In the exam, it is likely that you will be asked to argue a given topic. Here are two of the kinds of question you might be given:

1. Write an article for your local newspaper arguing either for or against a new housing development planned in your area.

2. Write to your MP arguing either for or against the idea of paying students to stay on at school or college after the age of sixteen.

Approaching the topic

The key to presenting an effective argument is to decide on the points you will make, both facts and opinion, then plan how you will structure and present them. Here is what you need to do:

Remember – effective planning is essential to success.

1. Think carefully about the topic you have been given.

2. Decide on your point of view.

3. Write down all the ideas you can think of **both for and against** the view you have taken.

4. Decide on the points you are going to make.

5. Arrange your points in a logical order that develops your ideas effectively.

6. Think about how you are going to support your ideas – what evidence you will use.

7. Decide how you are going to conclude your argument.

Structuring your argument

There are three basic parts to the structure of an argument.

1. **Introduction** – states the topic and explains your basic point of view.

2. **The main body** – presents your arguments in favour of your point of view; gives reasons for your opinion and supports them with facts and evidence.

3. **The conclusion** – sums up your ideas and reinforces your point of view. Make sure your final paragraph is strong and convincing.

How to plan, structure and write an argument of your own in answering an exam question.

Approaches

There are many ways you can tackle a question that requires 'writing to argue'. Two possible ones are:

1. A response in which you state one side of the argument and then counter with your own argument.

2. A response in which you write from your own viewpoint throughout but you also introduce alternative views in order to counter them with your own arguments.

You can use the same techniques to **write** arguments as to **analyse** arguments written by others (see page 6).

Remember that effective written argument requires:

- a forceful opening
- logical structure
- clearly-made points
- supporting evidence
- other viewpoints
- effective use of language
- a strong conclusion

Progress check

1. Why might repetition be used in an argument?

2. Name two places where you might find written arguments.

3. 'The number of cars on the road is increasing.' Is this a fact or an opinion?

4. 'Charging student tuition fees is a really bad idea.' Fact or opinion?

PERSUASIVE WRITING 1

The purpose of persuasive writing

The main objective of persuasive writing is to persuade the reader to do something, believe in something, or think something. There is some overlap with writing an argument, which is also trying to convince the reader – in that case to a particular point of view.

We encounter persuasive writing every day in our lives and it can come in all kinds of forms. For example:

- **advertisements** try to persuade us to buy the products they are advertising

- **charity appeals** try to persuade us to donate money to their causes

- **public service information** tries to persuade us to believe in certain ideas, such as eating healthily

- **party political information** tries to persuade us to vote for a particular political party

Analysing persuasive writing

All persuasive writing has a **purpose** and addresses a particular **audience**. This involves the use of various techniques. In the exam you might be asked to analyse an example of persuasive writing. To do this you need to be aware of the language techniques used to create effects. You might also be asked what effect is created. Some key techniques to look for are shown opposite.

What 'persuasive writing' means, its purpose, the techniques that writers use and how to write your own piece of persuasive writing.

10 MINS

DAY 1

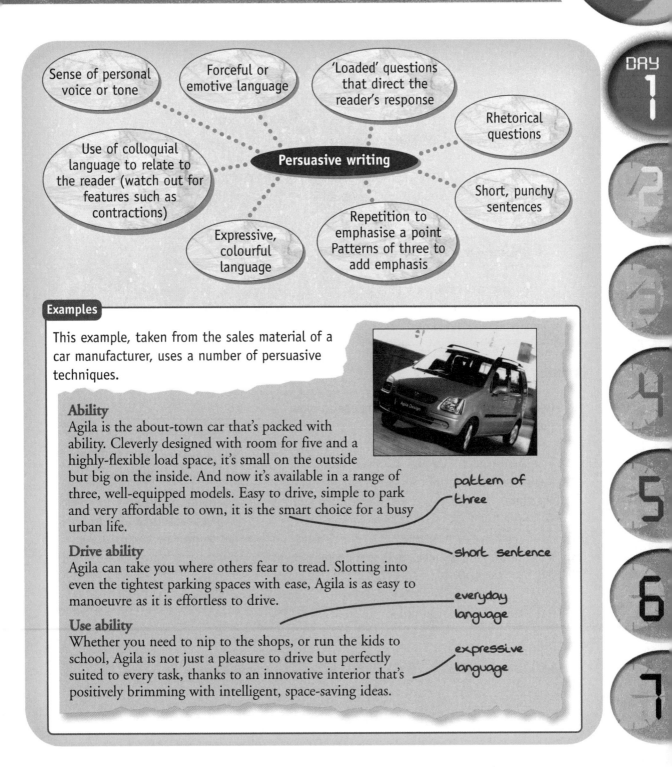

Sense of personal voice or tone

Forceful or emotive language

'Loaded' questions that direct the reader's response

Rhetorical questions

Use of colloquial language to relate to the reader (watch out for features such as contractions)

Persuasive writing

Short, punchy sentences

Expressive, colourful language

Repetition to emphasise a point Patterns of three to add emphasis

Examples

This example, taken from the sales material of a car manufacturer, uses a number of persuasive techniques.

Ability

Agila is the about-town car that's packed with ability. Cleverly designed with room for five and a highly-flexible load space, it's small on the outside but big on the inside. And now it's available in a range of three, well-equipped models. Easy to drive, simple to park and very affordable to own, it is the smart choice for a busy urban life.

pattern of three

Drive ability

Agila can take you where others fear to tread. Slotting into even the tightest parking spaces with ease, Agila is as easy to manoeuvre as it is effortless to drive.

short sentence

everyday language

Use ability

Whether you need to nip to the shops, or run the kids to school, Agila is not just a pleasure to drive but perfectly suited to every task, thanks to an innovative interior that's positively brimming with intelligent, space-saving ideas.

expressive language

Question types

In the exam there are two basic kinds of question that you might be asked:

1. One requiring a formal style, such as:

Write a letter to the leader of your local council to persuade him/her of the need to improve the recreational opportunities for young people in your area.

2. One requiring a more informal approach, such as:

Imagine that you are giving a talk to your class to persuade them to join you in organising a fund-raising activity for a charity. Write the speech you would make.

Planning

1. Decide on the **audience** and **purpose** for your piece of writing.

2. Decide on the level of formality needed and the **tone**.

3. Write down all your ideas and supporting points.

4. Put them into a logical order.

The opening – make it capture the reader's attention.

The main body – develop ideas clearly and use a range of techniques.

The ending – sum up what you have said in a persuasive way.

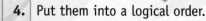

Techniques to use

- A personal tone that the reader can relate to.
- Emotive language to appeal to your audience's emotions.
- Rhetorical questions to make your points and encourage your reader to agree with you.
- Repetition to emphasise your points.
- Exaggeration, if it is appropriate (use sparingly).

What the examiner is looking for:

- awareness of audience and purpose
- use of appropriate tone and level of formality
- effective use of persuasive techniques
- clear structure
- technical accuracy

Progress check

1. Why is repetition used in persuasive writing?

2. What effect can be created through the use of informal language?

3. Fill in the missing words. 'All persuasive writing addresses an _____ in order to achieve its _____.'

4. What is emotive language?

5. What should the opening of your writing aim to do?

6. Your writing should end on a _____ note.

WRITING TO ADVISE 1

There are many kinds of advice on all kinds of topics.
Some of it we seek out for ourselves, some we are
offered through a variety of sources.

Example

Here is an example from the Road Safety Website. Look at it
carefully and think about the techniques used to make the advice effective.

THINK! Road Safety Website

▼ Think! Home | ▼ Road Safety Campaigns | ▼ Advice | ▼ Calendar | Contacts | Site Map

- Introduction
- Child road safety: parents
- Child road safety: teachers
- Child car seats
- Avoiding low bridges
- Couriers
- Cyclists
- Driving when tired
- Emergency vehicles
- Overseas visitors
- Mobile phones
- Motorbike riders
- Driving on motorways
- New drivers
- Older drivers
- Seat belts
- Teenagers
- Top ten tips
- Tyre safety

THINK! Home | Advice

THINK! advice - cyclists

Cyclists and drivers both have a right to use our roads - but sometimes you need to give a bit more thought to each other.

Dos and don'ts for cyclists

- Be visible. Ride well clear of the kerb, wear bright clothing and always use lights after dark or in poor weather conditions.
- Show drivers what you plan to do. Always look and signal before you start, stop or turn.
- Ride a straight line past parked cars rather than dodging between them.
- Don't jump red lights.
- Don't ride on pavements.
- Don't ride the wrong way up one-way streets, unless there's a sign saying cyclists can.
- Don't ride across pedestrian crossings.

Dos and don'ts for motorists

- Expect sudden movements by cyclists, especially in windy weather and on bad road surfaces.
- Watch for cyclists on the inside when you turn left.
- Always look for cyclists before opening a car door.
- Give cyclists turning right extra consideration.
- Don't squeeze past cyclists - give them space, at least half a car's width.
- Don't dazzle cyclists - use dipped headlights, the way you would with another car.
- Don't get annoyed when cyclists ride away from the kerb - they need to avoid drains and potholes, and be seen they come to junctions with side roads.

Our leaflet *Drive safe, cycle safe* for more advice. Visit our site for younger cyclists http://www.cyclesense.net for tips on staying out of harm's way.

How the use of language and layout can make advice clear and easy to understand and ways to approach 'writing to advise'.

10 MINS

A Striking title, clearly addresses audience.

B To the point introduction.

C Imperatives to make advice clear.

D Clear structure separates two sets of points.

E Clear and simple language to give advice effectively.

F Bullet points make text stand out.

G Advice on where to find more information.

Summary of techniques used:

- the language is clear and simple

- it has a clear, simple heading making the target audience clear

- it is divided up into clear sections, each dealing with a particular aspect

- bullet points are used to make each piece of advice stand out clearly

- imperatives are used to add force to the advice points

- information is included on where to find further advice

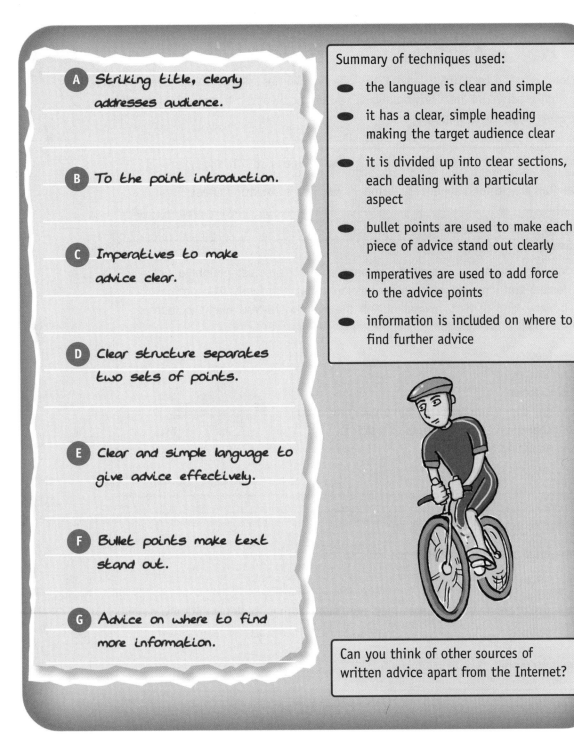

Can you think of other sources of written advice apart from the Internet?

DAY 2

Types of question

If you are asked to 'write to advise' the question will usually give you specific instructions on what exactly you are advising about. You might be asked to present your advice in different ways, for example:

- an information leaflet
- an article for a school magazine
- a letter to a friend
- an information sheet

Example

Write an advice leaflet aimed at people who have just bought a pet for the first time, advising on how to look after it properly. The pet can be any kind of bird, animal or fish that you wish. You might include information on:

- feeding
- housing
- exercise
- any special training/taming/handling required
- special problems/ailments to watch for
- grooming and bathing

What the examiner is looking for:

- clear awareness of audience and purpose
- effective planning
- use of techniques such as headings, subheadings, bullet points etc.
- effective presentation
- appropriate use of language

Approaching the question

1. Read the question carefully.

2. Be clear in your mind of your **purpose** in writing the advice.

3. Be clear in your mind about the **audience** you are writing for.

4. Plan what you are going to include in your advice.

5. Plan how you are going to structure it.

6. Think about the particular presentation techniques you are going to use, such as bullet points, headings, subheadings and questions.

7. Use language that is appropriate to your target audience.

8. Keep the text simple and to the point.

I'm trying to give up smoking. Any words of advice?

Yeah...

Put the cigarette in your mouth, but don't light it.

Right ... I hadn't thought of that.

'Writing to analyse' is an important element in your GCSE English course and you might be asked to use your analytical skills in a variety of ways. Your analysis might also be part of a wider task that requires you to 'review' and 'comment' as well.

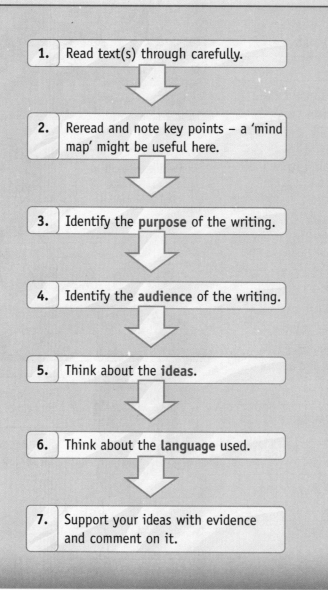

1. Read text(s) through carefully.

2. Reread and note key points – a 'mind map' might be useful here.

3. Identify the **purpose** of the writing.

4. Identify the **audience** of the writing.

5. Think about the **ideas**.

6. Think about the **language** used.

7. Support your ideas with evidence and comment on it.

A look at different kinds of analytical writing and ways of approaching tasks that require you to analyse writing or write your own piece of analytical writing.

10 MINS

DAY 2

You might be asked to:

- analyse the ideas on an issue or topic as presented by a writer

- analyse your own thoughts and ideas on a topic

- analyse the ways writers use language to convey their ideas

The kinds of texts that you might be asked to analyse might be:

- magazine articles

- extracts from books

- newspaper articles

- information from a website

- information leaflets

- advertisements

Kinds of question

Examples

A Read the following article carefully. (You will be given a text.) Analyse the writer's ideas and comment on how effective you find the article.

B Discuss your ideas and views on the issue of student loans.
Explain your ideas in detail and give reasons to support them

C Read the following extract carefully. (You will be given a text to read.) Analyse the ways in which the writer uses language to make the piece of writing effective.

DAY

2

○ Analysing a text

1.	Read it through very carefully, at least **twice**.
2.	Identify the **audience** and **purpose**.
3.	Write down the key points of **content**.
4.	Note down any examples of interesting use of **language**.
5.	Think about your **response** to the text and note any comments you might make.
6.	Structure your ideas in a **logical order**.

> **Content = what the text says.**
>
> **Language = how the ideas are expressed.**
>
> **Effect = the impact created by the text.**

○ Writing your analysis

Here are some points to think about in writing your analysis:

- What is the **audience**?
- What is the **purpose**?
- What is the **subject matter**?
- How is the piece **structured**?
- How is **language** used?
- How **effective** is the piece?

When writing about the language, remember to think about:

1. **Vocabulary** – pick out individual words and phrases and comment on their effects

⬇

2. **Syntax** – how sentences are structured

⬇

3. **Phonological** features – alliteration, assonance, onomatopoeia etc.

⬇

4. **Literary features** – imagery, simile, metaphor etc.

Remember: Make a point →

give an example →

comment based on the evidence

What the examiner is looking for:

● awareness of audience and purpose

● understanding of content

● analysis of language

● awareness of effects created

● clearly structured writing

Progress check

1 Name three possible types of texts you might be asked to analyse in the exam.

2 What is meant by the 'purpose' of a text?

3 What is meant by the 'audience' of a text?

4 What three key areas should you make notes on when preparing to analyse a text?

5 When you make a point, your ideas should be supported by _____ and _____.

6 What literary features could you look for in a text?

7 Analysing vocabulary involves picking out _____ and _____.

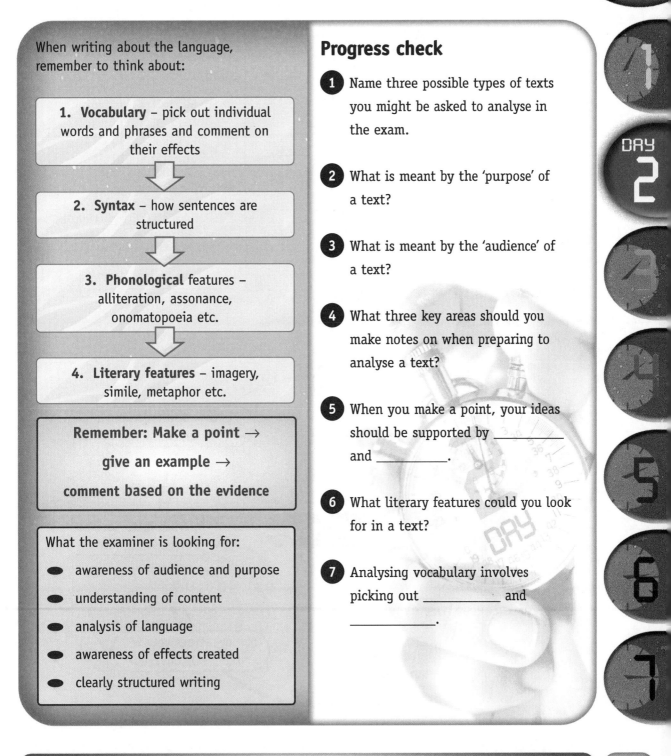

15 MINS

DAY 2

A review examines something and gives an opinion or assessment of it. For example, reviews could be written on:

- books
- plays
- TV programmes
- films
- music albums
- concerts or gigs
- exhibitions
- various consumer products
- holidays

In the exam you might be asked to:

- read reviews written by others, analysing them and commenting on their features and effects
- write a review of your own
- read material that you are given and review its content, style and effectiveness

○ Reading and writing about reviews

Here are some things to ask yourself when reading a review written by someone else:

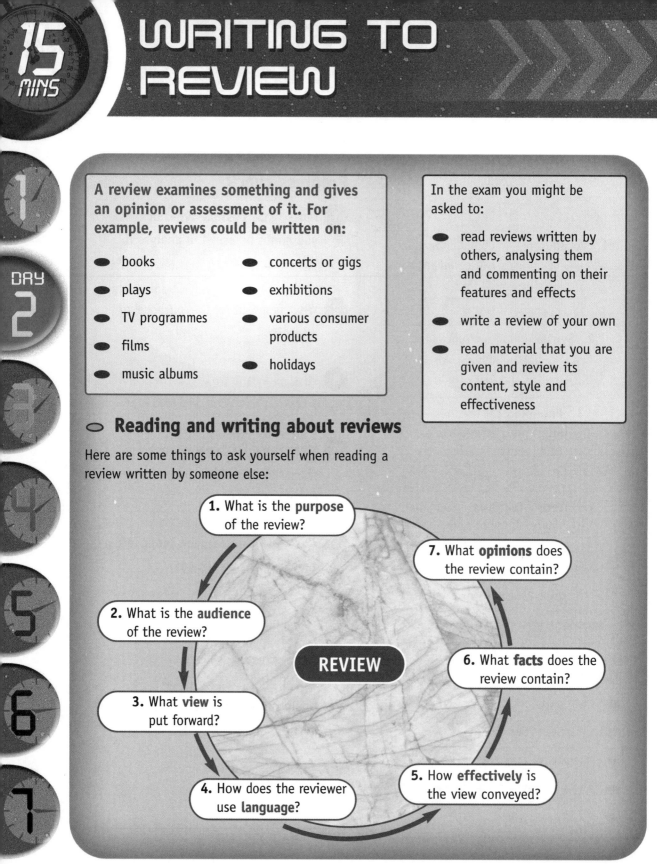

1. What is the **purpose** of the review?
2. What is the **audience** of the review?
3. What **view** is put forward?
4. How does the reviewer use **language**?
5. How **effectively** is the view conveyed?
6. What **facts** does the review contain?
7. What **opinions** does the review contain?

REVIEW

When writing your own review you should:

- plan your review carefully
- understand the difference between **fact** and **opinion**
- structure your ideas in a logical way
- make specific comments, not vague generalisations
- develop your ideas logically
- support your ideas and views

What the examiner is looking for:

- clear focus on task
- awareness of audience and purpose
- awareness of ways ideas are expressed
- understanding of the ways language is used
- analysis supported by example and/or evidence
- clearly structured response

Progress check

1 What does a review do?

2 When reading a review for the first time you should begin by identifying its _____ and _____.

3 When reading a review, it is important to distinguish between _____ and _____.

4 Name two types of review that you might encounter.

5 When analysing a review you should pick out specific features of _____ and comment on the _____ they create.

6 What are the three tasks involving 'writing to review' that you might be given in the exam?

DAY 2

WRITING TO COMMENT

'Writing to comment' can take several forms:

● you might be asked to comment on the ideas expressed in a text

● you might be asked to comment on how a writer uses language to create effects

● you might be asked to comment on your findings after you have analysed and reviewed a piece of writing

Many newspapers include a 'comment' column which expresses the particular view taken by the newspaper or columnist. Magazines often begin with a comment from the editor. These kinds of comments:

● express a view, an idea or an issue

● give an overview of the issue

● give a balanced comment

Example

Here is a piece of writing that comments on an issue. It is from a letter to a national newspaper:

Sir,

I would like to comment on a letter published last week in your paper suggesting that soft drinks, crisps and chocolate vending machines should be banned. I agree entirely with the writer's view that schools should not be seen to be promoting, or worse still, making money from selling food and drink that is harmful to health. We are constantly told these days of the problems to health of excessive sugar and fat intake and so we should do more to encourage healthy eating in schools rather than the consumption of junk food.

This begins with a clear statement of what is being commented on.
There is a straightforward comment which states the writer's view.
Further comments develop from this.

The forms 'writing to comment' can take, how to comment on texts and ideas and what types of questions might be asked.

Types of question

In the exam, it is likely that a question asking you to comment will be part of a broader task requiring you to analyse as well. For example, you might be given an article to read and then asked to:

- analyse the way the writer uses language to express his/her ideas
- comment on how far you agree with the views expressed

Approaching the task

- Make your comments balanced.
- Make your comments relevant.
- Explain your ideas clearly.

What the examiner is looking for:

- clear expression of ideas
- evaluation of written source material
- analytical points
- evidence to support points made
- structured response

Progress check

1. Name three things you might be asked to comment on in the exam.

2. What kind of publication has a 'comment' column?

3. To what other kinds of writing might 'writing to comment' be linked?

4. Your comments should be _____ and _____.

5. What three forms could 'writing to comment' take?

The purpose of 'writing to inform' is to give the reader information as clearly and effectively as possible. Informative writing gives details, facts and information. 'Writing to inform' can vary a great deal depending on the kind of information that is being given and the audience it is aimed at. Informative writing can be presented in many forms, including:

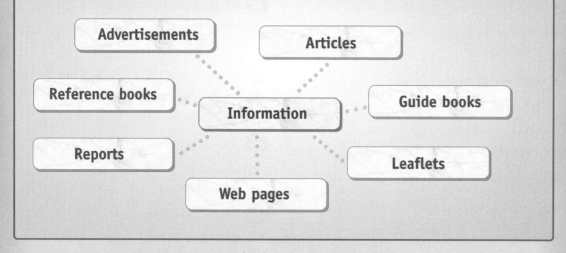

Advertisements
Articles
Reference books
Information
Guide books
Reports
Leaflets
Web pages

Whatever form it takes, informative writing **always**:

- uses clear and straightforward language

- contains factual content

- gets straight to the point

- structures ideas logically

● Types of question

1. Write an information leaflet informing tourists about an attraction in your area.

2. Write an article aimed at an audience of your choice informing them of a subject about which you feel strongly.

Approaching the question

Identify your Audience.	Read the question carefully. Note the exact wording and use it to identify your audience.
List the key points you want to tell the reader.	Identify the specific information you want to include.
Put them in the order in which you are going to deal with them.	A clear and logical structure is important.
Decide on how much detail.	This will be closely linked to your purpose.
Decide on how you are going to present your information.	Plan carefully and pay attention to techniques.
Make sure your information is clear and easily understood.	Use clear language and present ideas in a straightforward way.

What the examiner is looking for:

- writing suited to audience and purpose
- appropriate language
- clear structure
- effective presentation

DAY 3

10 MINS

DAY 3

Tasks involving 'writing to explain' can take many forms. Here are some of them:

- instruction booklets
- recipes
- directions to a particular place
- instructions on using equipment
- instructions on how to carry out a particular process

Example

Here are some instructions on introducing fish to a new aquarium:

Once fish have been introduced monitoring of the water quality should begin. Ammonia is the first waste product to accumulate followed by nitrite; both of these should be monitored weekly for the first 3–6 months to ensure levels stay within safe margins.

If the level of waste is increasing cut down on the amount of food and regularity of feeding and increase the number of water changes carried out. Water changes dilute any toxins and if necessary 30% of the water can be replaced every few days until the levels are safe. Always remember to use a dechlorinator.

Once these levels are stable preferably remaining at zero or close to it nitrate should be monitored. Fish are capable of tolerating low levels of nitrate but ideally it should not be allowed to accumulate to levels above 40p.p.m.

Regular tank maintenance should be sufficient to control water quality. Newly set up tanks should have 25–50% of the water

Why do new fish become ill? This is usually related to stress. Fish become stressed when they are handled and moved or if the concentrations of ammonia, nitrite or nitrate are too high. Fish that are already living in a tank will be tolerant of the water conditions that exist.

When new fish are added to a tank the sudden change they experience can have an adverse effect upon them and allow diseases to develop.

New fish should be observed very carefully for several days after they are introduced.

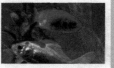

One of the most common problems faced by fish keepers is the development of whitespot in newly acquired fish. Whitespot is a tiny parasite that swims free during its infective stage;

Notice how the information is presented:

- clear and logical structure
- concise
- visual presentation makes it easy to understand

● Approaching the task

1.	Identify the purpose and audience.
2.	List the key points to be included.
3.	Put them in order.
4.	Decide how much detail you need.
5.	Think about how you will present it.
6.	Make everything clear.

'Writing to explain' involves conveying information logically and effectively, and how to approach tasks asking you to 'explain'.

● Types of questions

There are two basic types of questions:

1. explaining how to do something

2. explaining how you feel or felt about something

Examples

1. You are responsible for organising a day out for a group of students. Write an instruction leaflet giving them details of what they need to do. You should include information such as:
   - the date and time
   - the destination
   - what the programme for the day will be
   - everything they need to bring with them
   - what they might expect to do during the day out

2. Explain how you felt at an important moment in your life.

What the examiner is looking for:

● explanation suited to audience and purpose

● clear and accurate use of language

● clearly structured explanations

● appropriate presentation

WRITING TO DESCRIBE

When you are 'writing to describe' you should create a picture for your audience so that they can clearly and vividly imagine the scene, person or situation that you are describing. There are three important elements that you should think about:

- the opening – one that captures the reader's attention

- the ending – a dramatic moment; a revelation; an effective rounding-off of the description

- the language – careful choice of vocabulary and the way you use it

Example

Here is an example of the kind of question you might be given:

Describe the scene on market day in a town or city you know.

Here is one student's opening to this task:

With the exception of Sunday, no day is a quiet day in my local town. On market day, though, the activity and general bustle of the place moves up a gear. The open central square becomes transformed as the stalls with their brightly coloured canopies are erected, which gives the whole place a holiday atmosphere and today is no exception. The sun has brought the crowds out. Smells of burgers, hot dogs and fried onions drift in the air and the shouts of the market traders ring out as they announce their latest offers like town criers proclaiming the latest news. A small child tugs on his mother's arm, as excitedly as if it were Christmas, pointing to the huge balloons bobbing and blowing on their strings at the toy shop.

'Cheapest strawberries in town!' shouts the red-faced man on the fruit stall. 'Not as cheap as those in the shop in the High Street,' I hear an old man mumble as he passes by.

How to plan a piece of descriptive writing and make it vivid and effective.

How to make your writing vivid:

- draw on your own experiences about:
  - people you have met
  - situations you have been in
  - conversations you have heard
- use adverbs and adjectives
- use description that appeals to the five senses
- use various language techniques, such as:
  - simile
  - metaphor
  - alliteration
  - sentences of varying length

Remember: don't try to include every detail but capture the atmosphere.

What the examiner is looking for:

- effective use of descriptive language
- focus on the question
- use of imagery
- appeal to the senses

Progress check

1. What is the main purpose of writing to describe?

2. Name three important elements you should think about in 'writing to describe'.

3. What should the opening of your description do?

4. Name the five senses.

5. Name two techniques that you could use to make your description more vivid.

6. In writing your description you might be able to draw on your own _____, or _____ you have met, or _____ you have been in or _____ you have heard.

Kinds of texts

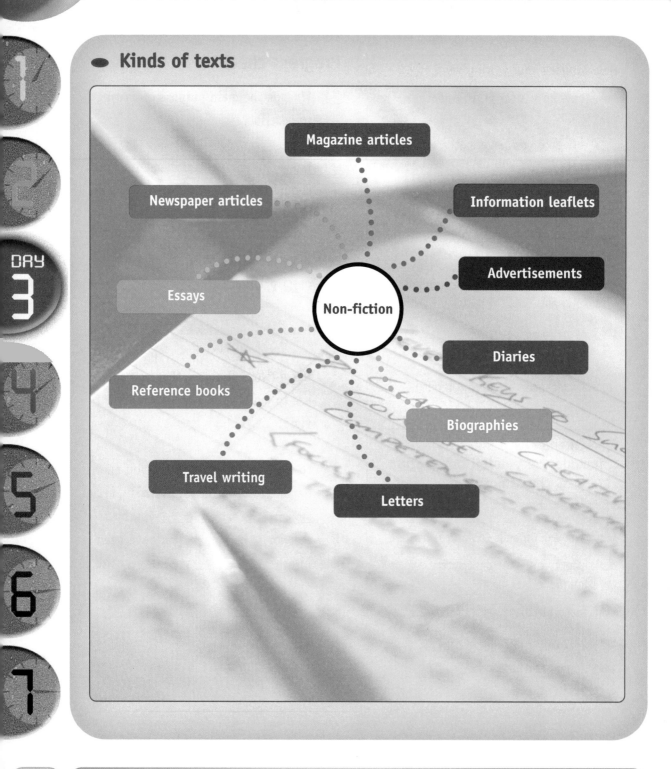

Magazine articles

Newspaper articles

Information leaflets

Advertisements

Essays

Non-fiction

Diaries

Reference books

Biographies

Travel writing

Letters

10 MINS

Purpose and audience

The **audience** and **purpose** of a non-fiction text can vary tremendously.
Non-fiction texts might:

- inform
- persuade
- advise
- comment
- describe
- entertain
- explore
- analyse

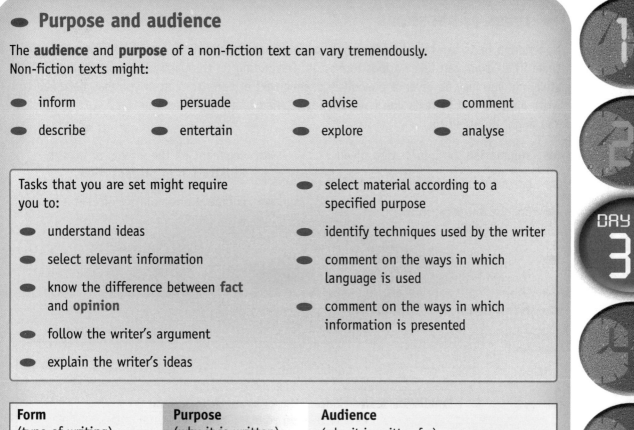

Tasks that you are set might require you to:

- understand ideas
- select relevant information
- know the difference between **fact** and **opinion**
- follow the writer's argument
- explain the writer's ideas
- select material according to a specified purpose
- identify techniques used by the writer
- comment on the ways in which language is used
- comment on the ways in which information is presented

Form (type of writing)	Purpose (why it is written)	Audience (who it is written for)
Leaflet on guinea pigs →	To inform →	Someone wanting a guinea pig as a pet
Recipe →	To instruct →	Someone wanting to cook a specific meal
Reference book →	To inform →	Someone wanting to look up a particular piece of information
Travel writing →	To describe/ entertain →	People with an interest in travel
Advertisement for holiday →	Persuade →	People who might be attracted to a particular resort
Film review →	Inform/persuade →	People interested in a particular film

DAY 3

Types of questions

Non-fiction texts can take a wide variety of forms, so the questions you might be asked about them in an exam can take various forms too. Depending on the particular course you are studying, you may be given a previously unseen text or texts to read or you may be asked to write about a text or texts you have already studied in a pre-release booklet.
You might be asked to:

- **summarise** the information given
- comment on the **purpose** or **audience**
- analyse the ways in which writers use **language**
- analyse the **effects** created through language
- comment on the effects of **layout**, **illustration** or **presentation**
- **compare** one non-fiction text with another

Approaching the task

Example

Here is an extract from a guide to London that a student has begun to annotate.

Opening metaphor captures attention

Metaphor

Addresses reader directly

Listing of attractions

London's a feast – indeed, there's so much to see and do that you might have to **restrain your appetite**. Just scan the skyline, and already you're spoilt for choice. In the City the **grey-ribbed** dome of St Paul's Cathedral encases the **haunting** Whispering Gallery. Nearby, the spire of St Brides rises in **wedding-cake** tiers above basement Roman ruins. Nelson on his column in Trafalgar Square presides over one of the finest art galleries in the world.

Whatever **you** choose in whatever order, make sure to give **yourself** enough time really to savour not only the major sights but also the joys of simple things, such as standing on Tower Bridge at dusk watching the **red-glinting** waters of the **eddying** Thames, or picnicking amidst the trees and grassland of Hampstead Heath, or eating roasted chestnuts on a **crisp** winter's day at the gates of the British Museum.

Ties in with initial metaphor

Use of adjectives

Adjectives

Writing about non-fiction texts can take a variety of forms.

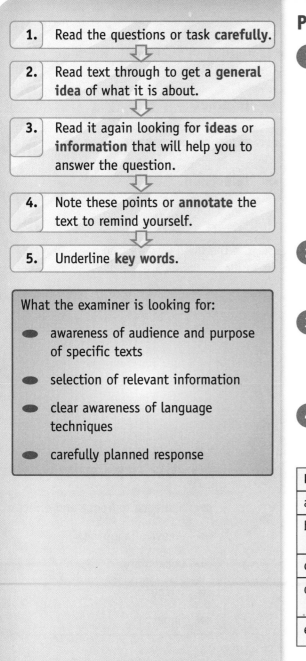

1. Read the questions or task **carefully**.

2. Read text through to get a **general idea** of what it is about.

3. Read it again looking for **ideas** or **information** that will help you to answer the question.

4. Note these points or **annotate** the text to remind yourself.

5. Underline **key words**.

What the examiner is looking for:

- awareness of audience and purpose of specific texts

- selection of relevant information

- clear awareness of language techniques

- carefully planned response

Progress check

1 Which of the following are non-fiction texts?

a) A short story.
b) A newspaper report.
c) An autobiography.
d) A novel.
e) An information leaflet.

2 Name three possible purposes of non-fiction texts.

3 What do you need to identify when first examining a piece of non-fiction writing?

4 Match the following forms of writing with the correct purposes:

Form	Purpose
a) Leaflet on a stately home	Entertain
b) Book describing a journey around Europe	Persuade
c) Advertisement for a car	Explain
d) Encyclopaedia entry on Romania	Describe
e) Recipe for chocolate cake	Inform

DAY
3

MEDIA TEXTS

DAY 3

What is the media?

'The Media' is the word we use as a general term to describe all the forms in which we convey information. This includes a range of things:

- **newspapers**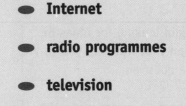
- **advertising**
- **magazines**
- **Internet**
- **radio programmes**
- **television**

Why is it important?

The media is very important in our society because it is the main way we find out about things – it communicates to us all kinds of ideas.

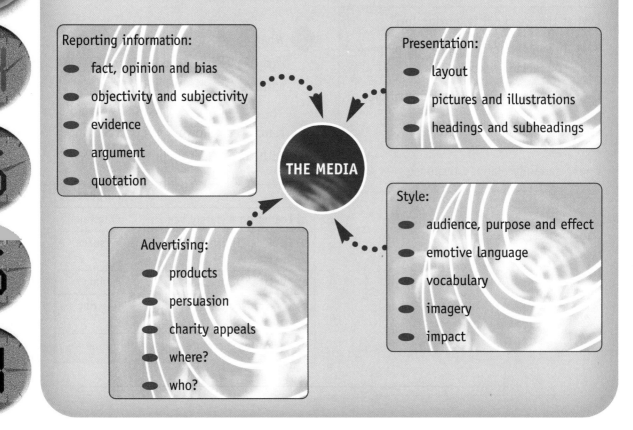

Reporting information:
- fact, opinion and bias
- objectivity and subjectivity
- evidence
- argument
- quotation

Presentation:
- layout
- pictures and illustrations
- headings and subheadings

THE MEDIA

Advertising:
- products
- persuasion
- charity appeals
- where?
- who?

Style:
- audience, purpose and effect
- emotive language
- vocabulary
- imagery
- impact

Checklist of features:

Layout and presentation

☐ photographs/images/drawings
☐ captions
☐ headlines and subheadings
☐ font size

Content

☐ fact
☐ opinions
☐ argument
☐ issues

Language

☐ vocabulary
☐ modifiers (adjectives/adverbs)
☐ technical/specialised terms
☐ verbs and nouns

Organisation

☐ sentences
☐ paragraphs
☐ punctuation

What the examiner is looking for:

● awareness of media types
● awareness of **audience** and **purpose**
● analysis of features

Progress check

1 Which of the following are 'media texts'?

a) poem
b) advertisement
c) television programme
d) short story
e) magazine article
f) novel
g) autobiography
h) newspaper report

2 What is the main purpose of the media?

3 What is emotive language?

4 Which four key features should you check for in a media text?

DAY 3

We see advertisements every day for a vast array of things, such as:

- food and drink
- holidays
- jobs
- political parties
- service trades
- charities
- public services
- goods of all kinds

They also come from a wide range of sources:

- television
- newspapers
- fliers through your letter box
- billboards
- radio
- magazines

Wherever they come from, however, they all have one purpose: to persuade you to behave or think in a particular way. The audience that adverts are aimed at can be very different.

Analysing advertisements

| 1. | Identify advertisement's **audience** and **purpose**. |

| 2. | To what is the advert trying to **appeal**? For example, conscience, fashion sense, health concerns or status. |

| 3. | Look at how the advert uses **headlines** or **slogans**. These key words are designed to be eye-catching. |

| 4. | Look at the visual techniques of **photographs**, **illustrations** or **logos**. What effect do they create? |

| 5. | Study the **language** used. Adverts make use of a wide range of language techniques to achieve their effects. |

An awareness of the language and visual techniques used in advertising will help you analyse and write about advertisements.

10 MINS

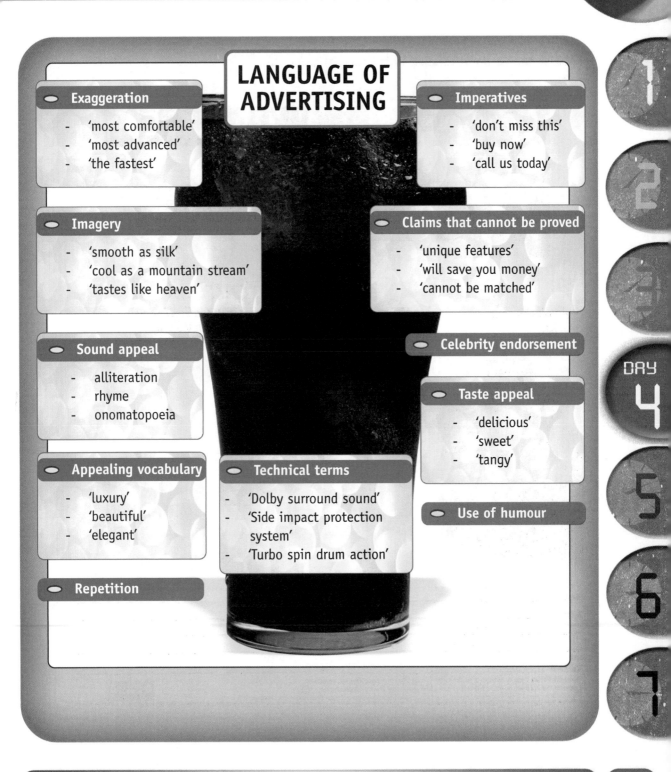

LANGUAGE OF ADVERTISING

Exaggeration
- 'most comfortable'
- 'most advanced'
- 'the fastest'

Imperatives
- 'don't miss this'
- 'buy now'
- 'call us today'

Imagery
- 'smooth as silk'
- 'cool as a mountain stream'
- 'tastes like heaven'

Claims that cannot be proved
- 'unique features'
- 'will save you money'
- 'cannot be matched'

Sound appeal
- alliteration
- rhyme
- onomatopoeia

Celebrity endorsement

Taste appeal
- 'delicious'
- 'sweet'
- 'tangy'

Appealing vocabulary
- 'luxury'
- 'beautiful'
- 'elegant'

Technical terms
- 'Dolby surround sound'
- 'Side impact protection system'
- 'Turbo spin drum action'

Use of humour

Repetition

DAY 4

Look at the techniques used in this advertisement.

The ULTIMATE lightweight vacuum cleaner

The Oreck XL7 is **so light and easy to use** that vacuuming on hard floors and carpets is a breeze, leaving you more time for the better things in life. Designed and engineered to last, it comes with an **amazing 7 year warranty.*** It is **energy efficient** yet **remarkably powerful,** removing and locking microscopic particles inside with its **HEPA standard filtration system.** Recently independently **rated as 'excellent' at pet hair removal,** you can be sure your flooring will be left beautifully clean, even deep into the carpet pile.

Worth £129!

Yours FREE
with purchase **Deluxe Compact Canister Vacuum - perfect for the car**

Combines with the XL7 to complete your vacuuming system. Includes 8 attachments.

ORECK®
XL7

30 Day Home Trial
Don't just take our word for it. Try it in your own home risk-free.

For further information please call FREE
0800 869 669
www.oreck.co.uk

OR fill in the coupon below and return to:
Oreck UK, FREEPOST (SWB30675), Exeter, EX2 8BF
We will pay the postage - you don't need a stamp. No sales person will visit.
*Warranties apply to domestic use only. Calls may be monitored or recorded for training purposes.

Name: _____
Address: _____
_____
_____ Postcode: _____
Tel.Day: _____ Eve: _____

Please tick this box if you do not wish to receive further special offers from companies we recommend. ☐
Please tick this box if you do not wish to receive information about other Oreck products or offers. ☐
©2004 Oreck Holdings L.L.C. All rights reserved. All words, marks and configurations are owned and used under the authority of Oreck Holdings L.L.C

AA45A

Range of features used:

- eye-catching headline: ULTIMATE
- offer of free equipment
- key phrases highlighted
- appealing words – amazing, efficient, remarkably powerful, excellent
- Technical terms: HEPA Standard filtration system, independent laboratory text, microscopic particles
- emphasis on warranty
- photograph emphasising lightweight quality
- 30-day home trial
- close-up photograph of vacuum cleaner in stylish, light room

What the examiner is looking for:

- awareness of purpose of advertisement
- awareness of potential audience
- discussion of visual techniques used
- analysis of language techniques used
- assessment of overall impact

The main purpose of newspapers is to report news but there are many different kinds of newspapers and many different kinds of news and ways of reporting it.

Types of newspaper	Content
Dailies, morning, evening	Sold every day and reporting up-to-date news; also contain information items and features.
Weeklies	Sold weekly and usually aimed at a particular town, section of a city or area of the country.
Sunday papers	Sold on Sundays and designed for more leisurely reading, with current news, review of previous week's news and many features; often include a colour magazine.
Free press/ advertisers	Delivered weekly to homes in one area; contains local news only and lots of advertisements.

Understanding and analysing the different kinds of material that can be included in newspapers.

Newspaper content

National news

World news

Local news

Political news

Horoscopes/crosswords

Sports news

Newspaper content can be very broad and varies with the kind of paper produced.

Comment sections

Interviews

Advertising

Entertainment

Reviews (films, theatre, music, TV)

Human interest stories

TV listings

Problem pages

Gossip columns

In addition to presenting news, newspapers also:

comment on events → make judgements on them
→ give opinions

DAY 4

The writers of the newspaper stories and articles shape the effect of their material in a variety of ways:

- headlines and sub-headings
- opinion and comment
- choice of language
- tone
- editing of information
- photographs and illustrations.
- presentation of facts

Example

Friday, June 4, 2004   PAGE 27

STUR CRAZY

Fisherman caught up in row over 10ft sturgeon

By RICHARD SMITH

A HUGE sturgeon landed fisherman Robert Davies in big trouble yesterday – even though he had the Queen's approval to sell it.

He was told he faced six months in jail or a £5,000 fine after police swooped on him at a fish market.

They said the the 10ft, 300lbs sturgeon was a protected species and impounded it.

Yet he had stuck to an ancient law insisting sturgeon is offered to the Queen. In a fax, the Palace said it was his and he sold it for £650 at Plymouth fish market.

Mr Davies, 38, of Llanelli, said: "I'm now regretting I didn't just throw it back."

But the South Wales Sea Fisheries Committee is backing his case: "It's a one-in-a-million chance of catching a sturgeon in Swansea Bay."

Sturgeon is usually found in the Caspian Sea.

richard.smith@mirror.co.uk

PRIZED: Robert's fish

Here are some comments from a student's analysis of this article:

- striking headline – play on words 'stir crazy'
- subheading – gives information that makes sense of headline
- use of word 'huge' emphasises fish's size
- 'Swooped' gives the impression of dramatic police action
- 'Impounded' adds to this impression
- mention of the Queen adds interest
- factual information, 'sturgeon is usually found in the Caspian Sea', given in final sentence
- photograph used shows size of fish and complements the text

What the examiner is looking for:
- awareness of purpose
- understanding of content
- understanding of layout
- attention to particular features, such as headlines and photographs
- analysis of language and effects

MEDIA PREVIEWS AND REVIEWS

Previews and reviews can be found every day in magazines, newspapers and websites.

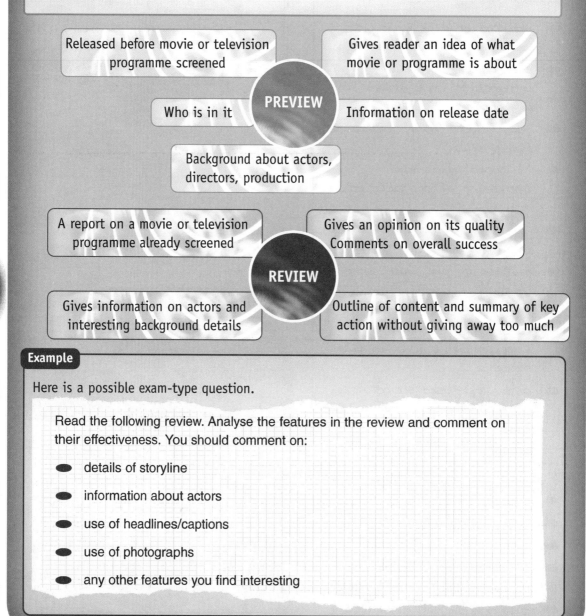

Released before movie or television programme screened

Gives reader an idea of what movie or programme is about

Who is in it

PREVIEW

Information on release date

Background about actors, directors, production

A report on a movie or television programme already screened

Gives an opinion on its quality Comments on overall success

REVIEW

Gives information on actors and interesting background details

Outline of content and summary of key action without giving away too much

Example

Here is a possible exam-type question.

Read the following review. Analyse the features in the review and comment on their effectiveness. You should comment on:

● details of storyline

● information about actors

● use of headlines/captions

● use of photographs

● any other features you find interesting

The function of movie and television previews and reviews and how moving images are presented.

15 MINS

THE DAY AFTER TOMORROW

STARRING: Dennis Quaid, Emmy Rossum, Jake Gyllenhaal, Ian Holm and Sela Ward
DIRECTOR: Roland Emmerich
RELEASE DATE: 28 May 2004
DISTRIBUTOR: Twentieth Century Fox
CERTIFICATE: 12A

When you notice that this film was written and directed by Roland Emmerich – producer of such classics as 'Independence Day', 'Godzilla' and 'The Patriot' – you know you're in for a thrilling adventure of a movie – not light on effects either. 'The Day After Tomorrow' lives up to the expectations set by his previous works in no short measures.

The movie premise in a nutshell is thus: What would happen if global warming continued at its current levels? The answer according to this film is a worldwide, catastrophic disaster of Biblical proportions. And when I say Biblical, it's no exaggeration – we're talking Hurricances, Tornadoes, Earthquakes, Tidal Waves, Floods and the beginning of the new Ice Age.

In the midst of all this chaos is the story's main character – Professor Adrian Hall (Quaid). Hall is a paloclimatologist – a scientist of weather patterns to you and me – and he is trying to save the world from the many catastrophes that have hit, and more that are to come. At the same time as doing this, he's also trying to track down his son, Sam (Gyllenhaal), who was visiting New York at the exact time that it was immersed in the beginnings of a North-American Ice Age.

As if this didn't sound hard enough, Hall's job is made even tougher by the fact that he is almost the only man heading North – everybody else is aiming for warmer climates in the southern hemisphere.

The actors put in fine performances here, but the real stars of the movie are the amazing special effects sequences, laid out in all their terrifying glory.

This is a great film, and one with a very real mesage too – reduce global warming or face the consequences in the future. Sadly, this message may be lost on a lot of the audience, particularly in America where a large proportion of the populace don't believe in 'global warming'. However, even if just one person is moved to act by this film it will have done a good job.

1
2
3
DAY 4
5
6
7

HOW TO USE THE QUIZ CARDS

There are several stages to successful revision – one of the most important is writing a list of the topics you need to know.

Then it's all about working through these essential topics, making useful notes and learning the key facts.

This is where these quiz cards can help you.

The questions on the cards provide a last-minute check of some key GCSE facts.

- You can leave them in the book and refer to them when you want

- You can tear them out and keep them handy for testing yourself

- You can get someone else to test you

- You can test your friends, which is also a good way of helping information sink in

- You can add to the cards by making your own sets of questions and answers

Remember – **PREPARATION** and **PRACTICE** and you'll be on the way to a good result!

Name the different elements that make up a story.

In an exam, how might you be asked to 'write to review'?

Name six things to look for in written argument.

Name three kinds of writing which could inform.

The structure of your argument should consist of three basic parts. What are they?

What language techniques could you use when writing an argument?

The use of what kind of parts of speech could make your writing more vivid?

Name four ways you might be asked to present advice.

Name four kinds of things that we might think of as being 'the media'?

What three ways might you be asked to 'write to analyse'?

Name four places where you might encounter adverts.

'Write your own review of a book, film or other material.' 'Write an analysis of a review written by someone else.'	Plot, characters, setting, structure, atmosphere, style, vocabulary.
Guidebooks, leaflets, advertisements, reference books, reports, webpages.	Facts, opinions, bias, emotive language, rhetorical questions, repetition.
Adverbs and adjectives.	Introduction, main body and conclusion. Factual information, opinions, emotive language, repetition and rhetorical questions.
Newspapers, magazines, radio programmes, advertising, Internet, television.	An information leaflet, an article for a school magazine, a letter to a friend, an information sheet.
Newspapers, magazines, television, cinema, billboards, flyers.	'Analyse the ideas on an issue or topic.' 'Analyse your own thoughts and ideas.' 'Analyse language.'

Name five kinds of newspaper.

What features might you find in pre-1914 poetry that you are less likely to find in post-1914 poetry?

Name three different kinds of camera shot.

What subject matter does modern poetry often deal with?

What kind of language does modern poetry often use?

What is blank verse?

What particular language techniques might a poem from other cultures contain?

What might you do to help you revise about the characters in a novel?

What must you **not** do when comparing poems?

What is assonance?

What can rhythm add to a poem?

Which of these words are misspelt?

wolen	Wedensday
independant	weird
murmur	category
seperate	
success	

Archaic language. Ideas that relate to a particular historical period. Unfamiliar references. Different spellings.

Dailies, weeklies, evening, Sunday, free.

Ideas and issues relating to life and relationships in the modern world.

Informal or conversational.

Cutting, close-up, long shots, panning.

Use of non-standard English, dialect/accent, phonetic spelling, names of places, ideas, beliefs and things relating to that particular culture.

Verse that doesn't rhyme – has a regular rhythm pattern with ten syllables per line consisting of a stressed syllable followed by an unstressed syllable.

Write all about one poem and then all about another, or write about one and then write about the other and just include a short paragraph comparing them at the end.

Draw up tables listing their key features with page references and quotations.

---

wolen = woollen, independant = independent, seperate = separate, Wedensday = Wednesday, categery = category

---

Repetition of a vowel sound.

A sense of movement or pace, helping to create mood and atmosphere.

EHAM TECHNIQUE

IN THE EXAM ITSELF...

- Follow all the instructions in the exam paper
- Attempt the correct number of questions
- Read each question carefully and more than once

FOLLOW OUR CHECKLIST TO HELP YOU BEFORE AND DURING THE EXAMS

- Highlight the key words in the question and note the command word – State, Describe, Explain, Discuss, Find, Suggest, Calculate, List etc.
- Check the number of marks available for each question and answer accordingly

Preparation

Use the time before the exams effectively. Write a list of all the topics you have to cover. Work through your notes systematically and ask for help with any topics that you're struggling to understand.

- Plan your response in brief note form
- Ensure that you answer the question asked and that your response stays relevant
- Allocate time carefully and make sure you complete the paper

Practice

Attempt as many practice questions and past papers as possible. Familiarise yourself with the question types, the marks allocated and the time allowed. Compare your marks to those given in the mark schemes – see where you did well and where there is room for improvement.

- Return to any questions you have left out and read through your answers at the end
- Remember that accurate spelling and good use of English do count

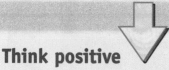

Think positive

Even if time is running short, remind yourself of the progress you have made. Use what time is left by working through the key topics – either those that are most likely to come up in the exam or those that you find most difficult.

We hope this book will help you on the way to GCSE success.

- Each individual image is called a **frame**.

- A series of frames is called a **sequence**.

- Moving from one shot to another is called **cutting**.

- Cutting from one scene to another for particular effects is called **montage**.

- Cameras are switched to show other people's reactions.

- **Close-up** shots move in close on the subject.

- **Long shots** pan back so the scene is viewed from a distance.

- Movie and television producers have a **purpose** and **audience** in mind.

Example

Here is a sequence from the soap *Coronation Street*. Look at each **frame** carefully.

Part of a student's analysis of these images:

Frame 1 shows Hayley, Fiz and Sonia with an expression of amusement and ridicule on their faces. We cannot yet see what they are laughing at, which builds comic tension. Frame 2 cuts to a close-up of Jack, wearing a woman's wig. The close-up allows us to see that he is clearly not as amused as the ladies to be looking so ridiculous! In Frame 3 the camera pans back to allow us to see Jack's full outfit, and his audience's amusement as he practises walking with a book on his head. In Frame 4, we cut to an outside shot of Jack strolling along in his amusing outfit, allowing us to see the street setting.

What the examiner is looking for:

- awareness of techniques and effects
- correct use of terminology
- discussion of how different effects can be created

Progress check

1 What is each individual image of a film called?

2 What does 'cutting' mean?

3 Why might close-up shots be used?

4 What term is used to describe the place where the action of a scene takes place?

5 What is the technique of moving the camera back for distance shots called?

6 Why might different camera angles be used?

DAY 4

READING SHAKESPEARE 1

Plot and structure

> **Plot – refers to the actual 'storyline' of the play**

> **Structure – refers to the ways in which the events of the story are put together.**

You need to know both the **plot** and the **structure** of the play you studied. Making a flow diagram will help your revision and make sure that you know when events happen and the order in which they happen.

> **Remember that your Shakespeare text is a play and is therefore meant to be seen on the stage.**

Characters

You can build up a picture of a character using different kinds of information.

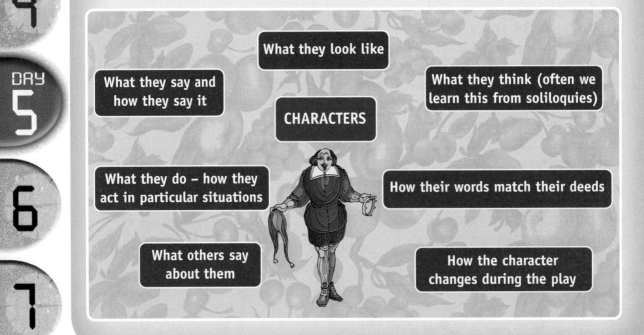

What they look like

What they say and how they say it

What they think (often we learn this from soliloquies)

CHARACTERS

What they do – how they act in particular situations

How their words match their deeds

What others say about them

How the character changes during the play

To revise for the Shakespeare play you have studied, you will need to understand plot structure, characters, themes, language and dramatic techniques.

A useful way to revise the characters is to create a character log for each of the main characters. Here is an example from one student's log on Tybalt from *Romeo and Juliet*.

Act/Scene	Character point	Evidence	Short supporting quotations	Lines
Act I, Sc 5	Aggressive – Tybalt sees Romeo and becomes angry	Orders servant to fetch his sword	'Fetch me my rapier, boy ...'	54
			'To strike him dead I hold it not a sin'	58

> When you make a point about a character, you should always provide evidence to back up what you say. A short supporting quotation is always useful too.

Themes

Every Shakespeare play has themes running through it. These are the ideas or issues that recur and develop as the play progresses. They are an important part of your study of the play because they contain the key ideas or messages that Shakespeare wanted to put across to his audience, so make sure that you know what they are. Here are some of the themes that Shakespeare deals with in various plays. Decide which are relevant to the play you studied.

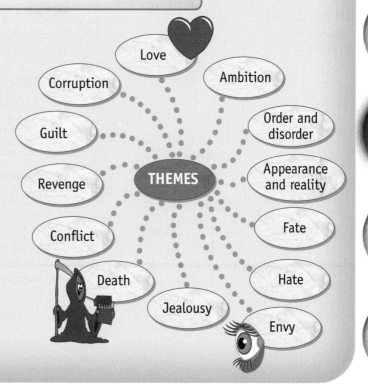

THEMES

Love
Corruption
Ambition
Guilt
Order and disorder
Revenge
Appearance and reality
Conflict
Fate
Death
Hate
Jealousy
Envy

Shakespeare's language

Language is at the heart of Shakespeare's plays so you need to be aware of the ways in which he uses it to create effect.

Poetry: blank verse

Most of the play that you have studied will be written in **blank verse**: it doesn't rhyme but it has a regular rhythm pattern. Each line contains ten syllables consisting of an unstressed syllable followed by a stressed one. This gives a 'ti tum ti tum ti tum ti tum ti tum' rhythm pattern. You can see this in the following line:

> But soft! What light through yonder window breaks?

This rhythm pattern closely resembles that of normal speech and lends itself effectively to dialogue. Shakespeare does use it flexibly, though, and alters it slightly sometimes in order to fit what he wants to say. He also uses **enjambment**, which is where one line runs on to the next.

Poetry: rhymed verse

Sometimes Shakespeare uses **rhyme** to create a particular effect, most often as **rhymed couplets** (pairs of lines that rhyme) to round off a scene or to emphasise a particular kind of atmosphere or situation. For example, the witches in

Macbeth usually speak in short couplets rather than blank verse:

> When shall we three meet again
> In thunder, lightning, or in rain?

Prose

Shakespeare also uses **prose** in some parts of his plays, most often for the minor or 'low' characters, but sometimes for major characters too. To find out why he uses it at a particular point in the play, you need to look at what is happening or being said just then that makes prose more appropriate than verse.

Imagery

Imagery is an important element in the plays. Look for:

- **Metaphors:**
  'There's daggers in men's smiles'

- **Similes:**
  'My bounty is as boundless as the sea'

- **Personification:**
  *'I think our country sinks beneath the yoke;
  It weeps, it bleeds, and each new day a gash
  Is added to her wounds'*

- **Antithesis:**
  'Fair is foul, and foul is fair'

Approaching the question

1. Identify clearly what the question is asking you.

2. Write your ideas down.

3. Make a plan.

4. Sort your ideas into paragraphs.

5. Link relevant quotes to points you make.

6. Expand your points through comment/analysis.

What the examiner is looking for:

- clear understanding of characters by the way they speak and act
- analysis of the language
- perceptive response to the question
- evidence from the text to support ideas
- well-selected references to support evidence

Progress check

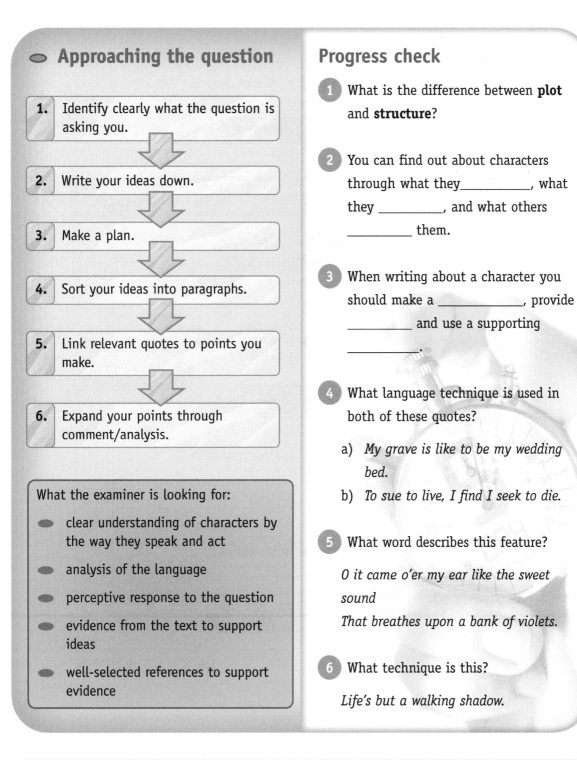

1. What is the difference between **plot** and **structure**?

2. You can find out about characters through what they_____, what they _____, and what others _____ them.

3. When writing about a character you should make a _____, provide _____ and use a supporting _____.

4. What language technique is used in both of these quotes?

   a) *My grave is like to be my wedding bed.*

   b) *To sue to live, I find I seek to die.*

5. What word describes this feature?

   O it came o'er my ear like the sweet sound
   That breathes upon a bank of violets.

6. What technique is this?

   Life's but a walking shadow.

DAY 5

TEST YOURSELF

53

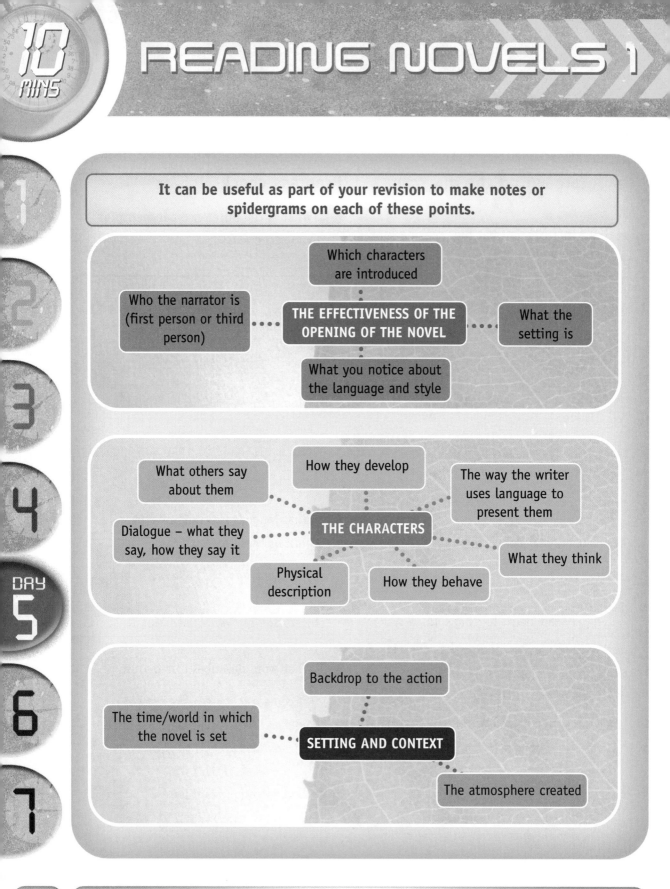

It can be useful as part of your revision to make notes or spidergrams on each of these points.

Which characters are introduced

Who the narrator is (first person or third person)

THE EFFECTIVENESS OF THE OPENING OF THE NOVEL

What the setting is

What you notice about the language and style

What others say about them

How they develop

The way the writer uses language to present them

Dialogue – what they say, how they say it

THE CHARACTERS

What they think

Physical description

How they behave

Backdrop to the action

The time/world in which the novel is set

SETTING AND CONTEXT

The atmosphere created

Some key points to revise for the exam on a novel you may have studied.

10 MINS

The ideas the writer explores

Attitude of the writer .... **THEMES** ... What the novel reveals about the themes

Effectiveness of the ending

What point does it make?

THE ENDING

What kind of ending?

Example

Here is one student's spidergram on the themes in the novel *Roll of Thunder, Hear My Cry*.

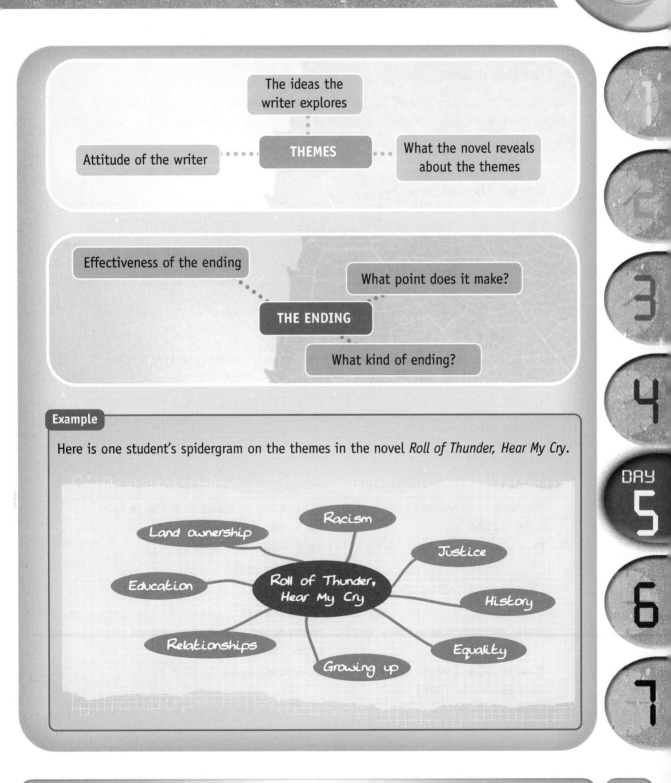

Racism

Land ownership

Justice

Education

Roll of Thunder, Hear My Cry

History

Relationships

Equality

Growing up

1
2
3
4
DAY 5
6
7

READING NOVELS 2

○ Making notes

Having identified the key themes in the novel, you can make more detailed notes on each of the themes with some examples of where the theme appears in the plot of the novel. For example:

Roll of Thunder, Hear My Cry

Theme	Where the theme appears	Page refs
Racism	The bus for white children. Black children have to walk.	Pages 21, 23, 27

Questions on characters are frequently based on the conflicts or contrasts between characters in a novel. As part of your revision it can be useful to draw up a table to list the similarities and differences between the main characters. Here is how one student made a table to compare Jack and Ralph, two characters in *Lord of the Flies*:

Jack	Ralph
Aggressive, insensitive (p34, 53)	Sensitive – concerned for others (p17, 19, 20) (p25, 32, 36)
Desire for leadership (p22)	Has sense of responsibility (p16, 21, 43)
Dictatorial (p35, 36)	Brave – stands up to Jack (p18, 27, 51)
Cruel/irresponsible (p56, 64)	Represents 'civilised' values (p15, 33, 62)
Destructive (p43, 50) Abuses power (p14)	Compassionate (p30)

Example

Here is an example of the type of question you might get in the exam.

How does Harper Lee present Scout's development in To Kill a Mockingbird?

Approaching the question

1. Read the question carefully and make sure you understand what it is asking you to do.

2. Jot down your main ideas.

3. Write a brief plan of what you intend to write.

4. Write your essay, remembering to use paragraphs.

5. Use short and relevant quotations to support your points.

6. Expand your points through comment/analysis.

What the examiner is looking for:
- sound knowledge of the text
- awareness of how characters are presented
- understanding of themes
- analysis of language use and effects

Progress check

1. What do you need to think about when looking at the opening of a novel?

2. When writing about characters you need to be aware of how the writer uses _____ to _____ them.

3. How else might you learn about the characters?

4. What is meant by the themes in a novel?

5. What is often a key element in the plot of a novel?

DAY 5

Approaching a short story

In many ways, studying a short story involves some of the techniques that you would use in studying a novel. You will need a clear understanding of the following:

Plot and structure: What happens in the story, the basic ideas, how the plot develops.

Narrative viewpoint: Who is telling the story? Is it told in the first or the third person? What effect does this have?

Characters: Who are they? How are they presented? How do they behave?

Language and style: How does the writer use language? What effects does this create?

Studying the story

1. Make a list of key events.

2. Look at the order in which these events appear.

3. Look at the time structure. Is it told in simple chronological order or does it use techniques such as 'flashbacks'?

4. Make a list of the characters and notes on how the writers present them, for example how they are described, what they do and what they say.

5. Look at the style in which the story is written, the language the writer uses and the effects it creates.

6. How does the story end? Is the ending left open? Is there an unexplained twist?

Beginnings

Compared to a novel, the opening of a short story must work very hard to engage the reader as there is less time to develop the story. Here are some possible ways in which short stories can open:

- the writer launches straight into the story
- the writer sets the scene by giving background information
- the writer opens with a dramatic word or phrase

Endings

- The ending may be left open.
- There may be an unexplained twist.
- The ending should have some kind of impact.

> What the examiner is looking for:
> - sound knowledge of text
> - understanding of narrative structure
> - understanding of writer's presentation of characters
> - awareness of how the writer uses language and the effects that this creates

Progress check

1 Look at this opening from a short story:

> I thought I knew you as well as I knew this house. No secret places, no hidey-holes, nothing in you I couldn't see. Now I realise how you kept yourself from me, how I didn't really know you at all.

Write down three ideas that this opening paragraph gives you about the story.

2 What is meant by the 'structure' of a story?

3 What is narrative viewpoint?

4 Name three things that you could consider when writing about characters in a story.

5 Why is the ending of a story important?

DAY 5

In your exams, you might be tested on three categories of poetry:

1. Pre-1914 (written before 1914)
2. Post-1914 (written after 1914)
3. Poetry from Different Cultures

All specifications require the study of Poetry from Different Cultures and some will also require the study of Pre-1914 or Post-1914 poetry. Make sure that you know what kind of poetry you are studying.

Poems are made up of different elements that are combined together to create the overall effect. Make sure that you know what all these elements are.

Form: the type of poem, for example sonnet, ballad or free verse.

Content: the subject matter, ideas and context dealt with in the poem.

Voice: the narrator who seems to be 'speaking' the poem. This might often seem to be the poet's own voice but sometimes the poet uses a **persona** (an adopted character).

Rhythm: often linked to the creation of a particular tone or atmosphere or sense of movement.

THE POEM

Tone and mood: closely linked to the 'voice' of the poem. The tone might be happy, sad, bitter, angry, thoughtful, etc.

Rhyme: used in different ways to create particular effects.

Imagery: a very important aspect of poetry which relates to the ways in which poets create a 'mental picture' in order to make the language they use more powerful and vivid.

Some ideas on how to approach your reading of poetry to prepare for the exam.

⊙ Approaching poetry

The first thing you should do when looking at the poems you are revising is to read each one and ask yourself the following questions about them:

1. **What** is the poem about? **Content**
2. **How** does the poet use language in it? **Style**
3. **Why** does the poet use language in that way? **Effect**

Once you have answered these broad questions, adopt a **planned** approach to add more detail to the study of the poem. It can be useful to annotate the poem.

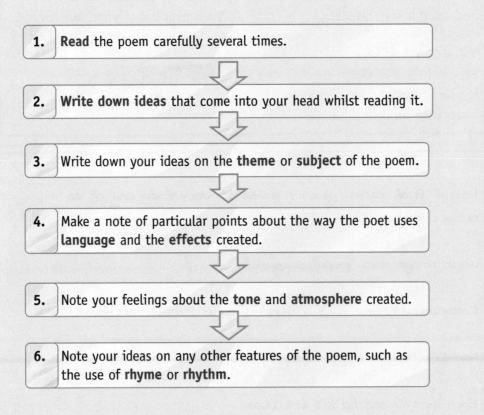

1.	**Read** the poem carefully several times.
2.	**Write down ideas** that come into your head whilst reading it.
3.	Write down your ideas on the **theme** or **subject** of the poem.
4.	Make a note of particular points about the way the poet uses **language** and the **effects** created.
5.	Note your feelings about the **tone** and **atmosphere** created.
6.	Note your ideas on any other features of the poem, such as the use of **rhyme** or **rhythm**.

Examples

Here are some annotations that a student made around Hardy's *The Man He Killed*.

'Had he and I but met[1]
By some old ancient inn,
We should have sat us down to wet
Right many[2] a nipperkin![3]

'But ranged as infantry[4]
And staring face to face,
I shot at him as he at me,[5]
And killed him in his place.

'I shot him dead because —[6]
Because he was my foe,[7]
Just so: my foe of course he was;
That's clear enough; although[8]

'He thought he'd 'list,[9] perhaps,
Off-hand[10] like – just as I –
Was out of work – had sold his
traps —[11]
No other reason why.

'Yes; quaint and curious[12] war is!
You shoot a fellow[13] down
You'd treat if met where any bar is,
Or help to half-a-crown.

1 Use of first person gives a sense of immediacy and of an authentic voice.

2 What image does 'many' suggest?

3 Colloquial word, meaning a drink, a small measure of spirits.

4 Narrative viewpoint is that of a soldier returned from the war.

5 Each was trying to kill the other.

DAY 6

6. Broken rhythm pattern reflecting soldier's struggle to what?

_____

7. What is the effect of repetition of 'foe'?

_____

8. Enjambment used for what effect?

_____

9. Short for 'enlist', i.e. join the army.

_____

10. Why 'Off-hand'?

_____

11. Belongings

_____

12. A detached and inadequate expression to describe a brutal event.

_____

13. Why 'fellow'? What are the connotations?

_____

Progress check

1. The word that describes the subject matter of ideas in a poem is

_____.

2. 'Voice' refers to the _____ of a poem.

3. Name two forms of poetry.

4. Why is imagery important to a poem?

5. When reading a poem for the first time, you should ask yourself _____ it is about, _____ the poet uses _____, and _____ it is used in that way.

IMAGERY IN POETRY

Poets use imagery to create a 'mental picture' of the thing or idea that is being described or explored. Sometimes imagery is called **figurative language**. Here are the key types of imagery you should be able to identify and discuss:

Simile: directly compares one thing to another as a description. They are easy to spot because of the use the words 'like' or 'as'. For example:

> Blackberries / Big **as** the ball of my thumb

or

> He watches from his mountain walls
> And **like** a thunderbolt he falls

Metaphor: a description which is not meant to be taken literally. Metaphors are similar to similes in that they also create a comparison but instead of saying something is 'like' or 'as' something else, metaphors say it **is** that thing. For example, the black birds in the poem below are compared to bits of burnt paper:

> Overhead go the **choughs** in black, cacophonous flocks
> **Bits of burnt paper** wheeling in a blown sky.

Personification: a description in which an animal, object or idea is referred to as if it were human, or is given human attributes. For example:

> I sift the snow on the mountains below,
> And their great **pines groan aghast**

SPEND 15 MINUTES ON THIS TOPIC

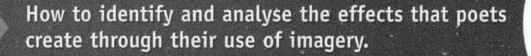

How to identify and analyse the effects that poets create through their use of imagery.

Wordsworth uses all three of these features in his sonnet *Upon Westminster Bridge*:

Earth has not anything to show more fair:

Dull would he be of soul who could pass by
A sight so touching in its majesty:

This City now doth, **like a garment, wear**
The beauty of the morning: silent, bare,
Ships, towers, domes, theatres, and temples lie
Open unto the fields, and to the sky;
All bright and glittering in the smokeless air.
Never did sun more beautifully steep
In his first splendour, valley, rock or hill;
Ne'er saw I, never felt, a calm so deep!
The river glideth at **his own sweet will**:

Dear God! the very houses seem asleep;
And all that mighty **heart is lying still**!

Simile: He says the beauty of the morning is 'like a garment' or article of clothing.

Personification: The sun is described as if a person 'In his first splendour'. The river is also described as a living thing with 'his own sweet will'.

Metaphor: The city is described as a 'heart lying still'.

AURAL IMAGERY

15 MINS

As well as creating imagery through words, poets sometimes use images that are created through sound – this is called aural imagery. There are several key techniques that poets use to create effects through sound.

Alliteration

This is when words next to, or close to, each other begin with the same consonant letter. For example:

> What would the world be, once bereft
> Of wet and of wildness?

Here, the repeated 'w' sound can give an impression of the wind blowing.

It's easy to spot in a poem, but why do poets use it? It can:

- create a sense of rhythm
- help to create tone
- draw attention to particular words

Assonance

This is when a vowel sound is repeated for effect. For example:

> Summer grows old,
> cold-blooded mother

Here the long, drawn out 'o' sounds create a slow, cold impression in keeping with the summer ending and winter approaching.

1
2
3
4
5
DAY
6
7

How to identify and analyse the effects that poets create through sound.

Onomatopoeia

This is when a word sounds like the thing it describes: 'bang', 'thud', 'hiss' are examples of this.

BANG

Rhyme

- Creates a musical quality or joining effect.
- Emphasises certain words.
- Draws lines together.
- Links ideas and images.

Rhythm

- Creates a particular sense of movement, such as liveliness or sluggishness.
- Can contribute to the creation of mood and atmosphere.

What the examiner is looking for:

- analysis of language and effects
- knowledge of literary techniques and terms
- clear understanding of poetic technique

Progress check

1. What is another term for imagery?

2. A simile _____ one thing to another, usually using the words _____ or _____.

3. What does personification mean?

4. _____ is when words next to, or close to each other, begin with the same consonant.

5. When a word sounds like the thing it describes, it is called _____.

6. Name four things that rhyme can create in a poem.

DAY 6

15 MINS

1
2
3
4
5
DAY 6
7

You should treat pre-1914 poems just like any others. However, you may come across features in them that you do not find in more modern poetry, for example:

- old-fashioned words: **archaic language**
- ideas that relate to the historical period in which it was written
- particular references that you might need to look up to fully understand them
- spellings that differ from modern English

Example

Here's how one student began to approach the following question. She began by annotating the poem, and marking each line to show the rhyme scheme.

Read the following poem carefully. How does Shakespeare explore his ideas about love and deception?

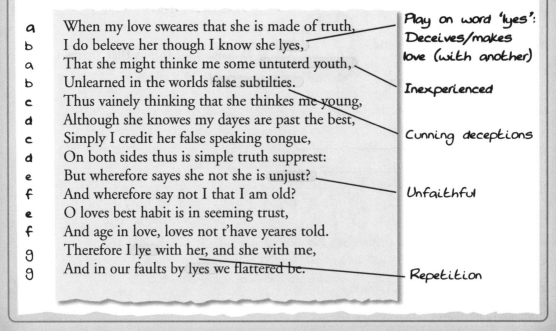

Sonnet form

a   When my love sweares that she is made of truth,
b   I do beleeve her though I know she lyes,
a   That she might thinke me some untuterd youth,
b   Unlearned in the worlds false subtilties.
c   Thus vainely thinking that she thinkes me young,
d   Although she knowes my dayes are past the best,
c   Simply I credit her false speaking tongue,
d   On both sides thus is simple truth supprest:
e   But wherefore sayes she not she is unjust?
f   And wherefore say not I that I am old?
e   O loves best habit is in seeming trust,
f   And age in love, loves not t'have yeares told.
g   Therefore I lye with her, and she with me,
g   And in our faults by lyes we flattered be.

Play on word 'lyes': Deceives/makes love (with another)

Inexperienced

Cunning deceptions

Unfaithful

Repetition

Some points to remember and think about when revising pre-1914 poetry.

15
MINS

Having annotated the poem, the student then quickly planned how she was going to answer the question.

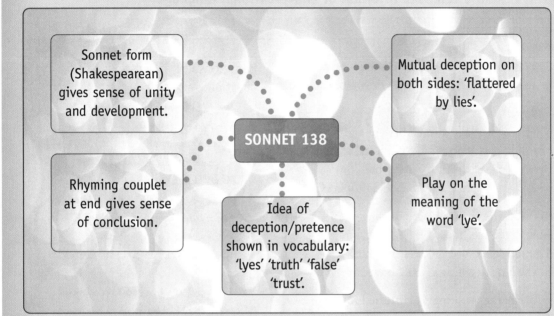

Sonnet form (Shakespearean) gives sense of unity and development.

Mutual deception on both sides: 'flattered by lies'.

SONNET 138

Rhyming couplet at end gives sense of conclusion.

Idea of deception/pretence shown in vocabulary: 'lyes' 'truth' 'false' 'trust'.

Play on the meaning of the word 'lye'.

The student then began her answer:

In this sonnet, Shakespeare explores the way that he knows he is being deceived by his lover but he misleads her too by pretending to believe her lies. He opens by pondering his loved one's lies to him and the way that she 'sweares that she is made of truth'. However, the poet makes it clear that, although he appears to believe her, 'I know she lyes'. The word 'lyes' implies a double meaning: she is telling him lies, and she lying down with someone else. His use of the word 'know' here gives a strong sense that there is no question in his mind about her unfaithfulness.

Modern poetry deals with ideas and issues we are more familiar with. It also often uses informal or conversational language.

Examples

Discuss the ways in which Heaney presents his relationship with his father in *Follower*.

Follower[1]
My father worked with a horse-plough,
His shoulders **globed**[2] **like a full sail strung**[3]
Between the shafts and the furrow
The horses strained at his **clicking tongue**[4].

An **expert**[5]. He would set the wing
And fit the bright steel-pointed sock.
The sod rolled over without breaking[6].
At the headrig, with a single pluck

Of reins, the sweating team turned round[7]
And back into the land[7]. His **eye**[8]
Narrowed and angled at the **ground**[8],
Mapping[9] the furrow exactly[8].

I **stumbled**[10] in his hob-nailed wake,
Fell sometimes on the polished sod;
Sometimes he rode me on his back
Dipping and rising to his plod. [11]

I wanted to grow up and plough[12]
To close one eye, stiffen my arm.
All I ever did was follow
In his broad **shadow**[13] round the farm.

I was a nuisance, tripping, falling,
Yapping[13] always. But today
It is my father who keeps stumbling
Behind me, **and will not go away**[14].

Here are some annotations on the question.

1. Why 'Follower'?
2. What image does the word 'globed' suggest?
3. Implies that his father is 'tied' to the plough.
4. A small sound, but one that has the power to command the horses.
5. An expert in his field.
6. What effect does this detail have?
7. An echo of the sailing simile.
8. Why might the poet have chosen to use rhymes and half-rhymes here?
9. What is the impact/implication of the word 'Mapping'?
10. The poet tried to follow in his father's footsteps, but clumsily.
11. Rhythm used to echo the action.
12. Wanted to be like his father but did not succeed – they have different skills.
13. Juxtaposition of the father's shadowy silence and the child's constant talking.
14. Although the roles are reversed, the son and the father are forever linked to each other. How?

Some points on how to revise the topic of post-1914, or modern, poetry.

The student then produced an essay plan:

Paragraph in essay	Stanza	Content
1	1 and 2	Image created of father: comment on effect of images
2 and 3	2 and 3	Effects created by descriptive detail
4	4	Focus switches to poet as a child: effect of this detailed picture
5	5	Childhood ambition
6	6	Reversal of roles
7		Conclusion, including significance of title

Remember – CLEAR and CAREFUL PLANNING is essential to a successful answer.

What the examiner is looking for:

- knowledge of poetic technique
- analysis of language and effects
- awareness of thematic explorations
- fluent and carefully planned response

You should approach poetry from other cultures as with all kinds of poetry and look at:

- the ideas and themes in the poems
- the ways the poems are structured
- the ways the poets use language and the effects they achieve

In addition, there are other things about the poems you will be expected to write about. These are to do with the features of the poems that make them culturally distinctive. These could include things such as:

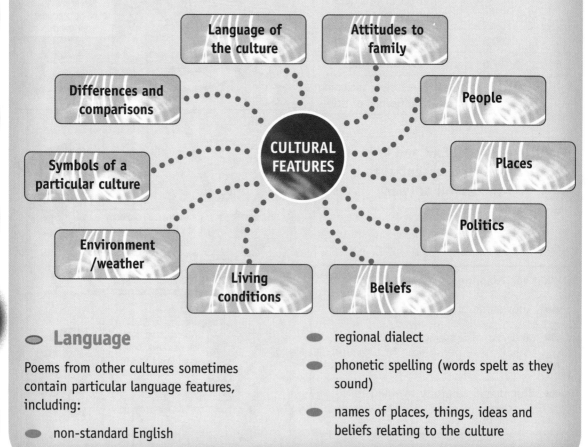

- Language of the culture
- Attitudes to family
- Differences and comparisons
- People
- Symbols of a particular culture
- Places
- CULTURAL FEATURES
- Politics
- Environment /weather
- Living conditions
- Beliefs

○ Language

Poems from other cultures sometimes contain particular language features, including:

- non-standard English

- regional dialect
- phonetic spelling (words spelt as they sound)
- names of places, things, ideas and beliefs relating to the culture

Some ways to approach revision of poetry from other cultures is an important element in GCSE English.

Example

The Song of the Banana Man

Touris, white man, wipin his face,
Met me in Golden Grove market place.
He looked at m'ol' clothes brown wid stain,
An soaked right through wid de Portlan rain,
He cas his eye, turn up his nose,
He says, 'You're a beggar man, I suppose?'
He says, 'Boy, get some occupation,
Be of some value to your nation.'
I said, 'By God an dis big right han
You mus recognize a banana man.

'Up in de hills, where de streams are cool,
An mullet an janga swim in de pool,
I have ten acres of mountain side,
An a dainty-foot donkey dat I ride,
Four Gros Michel, an four Lacatan,
Some coconut trees, and some hills of yam,
An I pasture on dat very same lan
Five she-goats an a big black ram,
Dat, by God an dis big right han
Is de property of a banana man.

Phonetic spellings

Small town in Jamaica

Tourism area near Golden Grove

Crayfish

Kinds of banana

Dialect forms

Writing in this way can:
- give the impression of a person 'speaking' the poem
- suggest an idea of character or persona
- create an impression of a particular culture

These responses are from students' essays in answer to the question of how the poems explore cultural differences.

● Symbolism and attitudes to family

Example

Here is an extract from *Presents from my Aunts in Pakistan* in which a girl living in Britain receives presents from Pakistan.

> They sent me a salwar kameez
> Peacock-blue,
> glistening like an orange split open,
> embossed slippers, gold and black
> points curling.

The presents that the girl were sent from her aunts in Pakistan are traditional garments worn by <u>Pakistani girls and women</u>¹. The salwar kameez, brightly-coloured loose-fitting trousers and the ornate gold and black shoes with curling toes are <u>symbolic of her culture</u>². It might be that her aunts want to make sure that she doesn't <u>forget her roots</u>³.

1. Identifies a key point straightaway.
2. Aware of symbolic significance.
3. Aware of attitudes of aunts.

● Politics

Example

This is an extract from *Not My Business*, which tells us something about the political climate of country in which it is set.

> They picked Akanni up one morning
> Beat him soft like clay
> And stuffed him down the belly
> Of a waiting jeep.

This poem is set in South Africa at the time of the abusive <u>apartheid</u>¹ regime. The <u>simile</u>² 'Beat him soft like clay' gives a vivid impression of the softness and fragility of his body and the strength of the beating. It also suggests that he was treated like an animate object³ 'stuffed' unfeelingly into the jeep; an act made more sinister as this <u>personified</u>² on the jeep as having a 'belly'.

1. Aware of political situation.
2. Imagery commented on.
3. Good awareness of effect.

Places and living conditions

Example

This is an extract from *Blessing*.

> The skin cracks like a pod
> There is never enough water.

Blessing is about the blessing of water in a country that is hot and dry[1]. These opening lines create a sense of the arid dryness through the image of the skin cracking[2] like the earth dries and cracks when there is no water. The simile[3] 'like a pod' adds emphasis to this sense of cracking open.

1. Awareness of place.
2. Links image with effect.
3. Simile/effect commented on.

1. **Make a point.**
2. **Support it with a brief quotation.**
3. **Comment on/analyse the effect.**

What the examiner is looking for:
- awareness of cultural themes in poems
- understanding of language use/effects
- understanding and analysis of poetic techniques

Progress check

1 What effects can the use of dialect/accent have in a poem?

2 Name **three** things that could make a particular culture distinctive.

3 On what aspects of the culture do you think these lines focus?

> I watched the holy man perform his rites
> to tame the poison with an incantation.

4 What do you think these lines show about the feelings of the speaker?
> I tried each satin-silken top –
> was alien in the sitting-room
> I could never be as lovely
> as those clothes –
> I longed
> for denim and corduroy.

5 What is the effect of the imagery describing a water pipe bursting in a country where water is scarce?
> ... The municipal pipe bursts,
> Silver crashes to the ground
> and the flow has found
> a roar of tongues.

COMPARING POEMS

Comparing **doesn't** mean: ✗	Comparing **does** mean: ✓
● writing all about one poem and then writing all about the other separately	● analysing both poems and showing their similarities and differences
● writing all about one poem then writing all about the other and then adding a short paragraph with some brief comparisons	● doing this throughout the response so that the comparisons are integrated

○ Planning your response

This is the type of question you might be given:

Explore the ways in which the relationship with a parent is presented in Poem A and Poem B.

1. Read both poems through carefully.

2. Make notes on the features of both poems, using a table like the one below.

	Poem A	Poem B
Content	Brief description of poem content	Brief description of poem content
Structure and effect	4-line stanzas. Rhyme: gives sense of formality and distance	Free verse: gives sense of informality
Language	Negative vocabulary. Little imagery used: effects created	Positive vocabulary. Metaphor and simile used: effects created
Tone and atmosphere	Pessimistic, negative tone	Optimistic, positive and loving tone

How to plan and write an effective comparison of two poems in your exam.

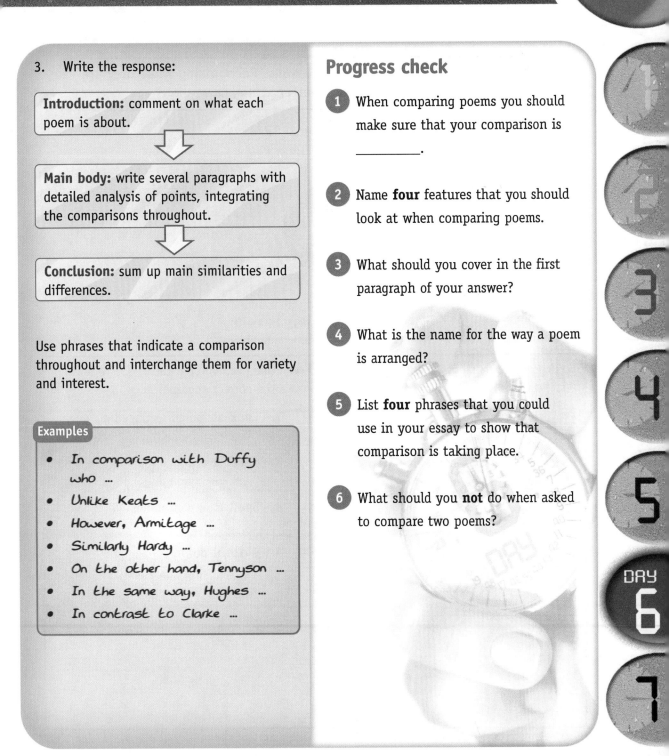

3. Write the response:

> **Introduction:** comment on what each poem is about.

⬇

> **Main body:** write several paragraphs with detailed analysis of points, integrating the comparisons throughout.

⬇

> **Conclusion:** sum up main similarities and differences.

Use phrases that indicate a comparison throughout and interchange them for variety and interest.

Examples

- In comparison with Duffy who ...
- Unlike Keats ...
- However, Armitage ...
- Similarly Hardy ...
- On the other hand, Tennyson ...
- In the same way, Hughes ...
- In contrast to Clarke ...

Progress check

1. When comparing poems you should make sure that your comparison is _____.

2. Name **four** features that you should look at when comparing poems.

3. What should you cover in the first paragraph of your answer?

4. What is the name for the way a poem is arranged?

5. List **four** phrases that you could use in your essay to show that comparison is taking place.

6. What should you **not** do when asked to compare two poems?

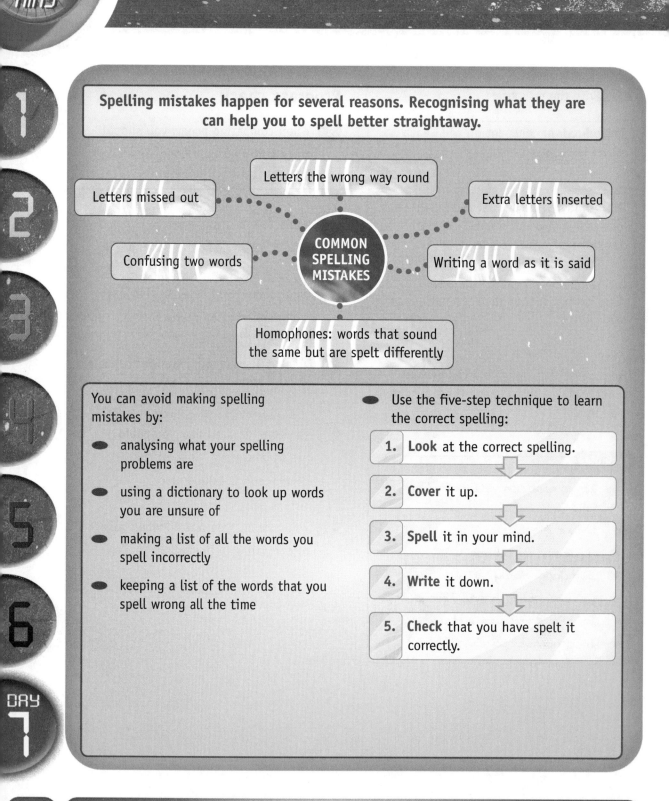

Spelling mistakes happen for several reasons. Recognising what they are can help you to spell better straightaway.

Letters the wrong way round

Letters missed out

Extra letters inserted

COMMON SPELLING MISTAKES

Confusing two words

Writing a word as it is said

Homophones: words that sound the same but are spelt differently

You can avoid making spelling mistakes by:

- analysing what your spelling problems are

- using a dictionary to look up words you are unsure of

- making a list of all the words you spell incorrectly

- keeping a list of the words that you spell wrong all the time

- Use the five-step technique to learn the correct spelling:

1. **Look** at the correct spelling.

2. **Cover** it up.

3. **Spell** it in your mind.

4. **Write** it down.

5. **Check** that you have spelt it correctly.

Help with spelling correctly, which is important both to make your reader understand your writing and to show your correct use of the English language.

10 MINS

Common spelling problems

Words ending in l

Full + fill = fulfil
Un + till = until
Awe + full = awful (**e** and **l** dropped)
Beauty + full = beautiful

> **Fill Till Full** = lose an 'l' when other letters are joined in front

Care + full = careful
Dread + full = dreadful
Fear + full = fearful
Harm + full = harmful

Double letters

Double letters can cause problems. Here is a way to sort them out.

1 In the alphabet, the letters called **vowels** are **a**, **e**, **i**, **o**, and **u**. the rest of the letters are called **consonants**.

2 Vowels can either have a **short sound**, as in thinner, rattle, putting, slotted and wettest. Notice that each **short vowel sound** is followed by a **double consonant**.

3 Vowels can also have a **long sound**, as in hike, later, meter, duty and motor. Notice how the **long vowel sound** is followed by a **single consonant**.

4 After a short vowel sound, double the consonant. After a long vowel sound, a single consonant follows.

A similar rule can be applied to the letters **ck**.

1 **Short** vowel sounds are followed by **ck**.

2 Bucket, locker, backwards.

3 **Long** vowel sounds are followed by **k**.

4 Hiking, baker, liking.

Plurals of nouns

Plurals can cause some confusion. The **general rule** when making plurals is to add an **s** but there are some exceptions and these can cause problems. The rules are:

1 Nouns ending in **s**, **ch**, **sh**, **x**, **z** and **o** = add **es** to make the plural.

bus = bus**es**, wit**ch** = witch**es**, rash = rash**es**, box = box**es**, topaz = topaz**es**, potato = potato**es**

2 Some nouns ending in **f** or **fe** change to **ves** to make the plural.

wi**fe** = wi**ves**, hal**f** = hal**ves**

3 Nouns ending in **y** change to **ies** in the plural.

country = countr**ies**, fly = fl**ies**

4 Some plurals **don't follow the rules**, and so you need to memorise them.

child = children, man = men, woman = women, mouse = mice, goose = geese

5 Some nouns **stay the same** in the plural.

sheep = sheep, deer = deer, fish = fish

6 Some nouns are **only used** in the plural form.

scissors, trousers, pliers

ie and ei

These two letters often cause confusion. You probably know the rule: 'i before e except after c', as in ceiling, receive and conceive. There are a number of exceptions to this; here are some of them:

- eight
- height
- leisure
- weigh
- either
- neighbour
- seize
- vein

Below are some pairs of words commonly misspelt because they are often confused with each other. Make sure you know the difference between these words:

- weather and whether
- quiet and quite
- new and knew
- past and passed
- principal and principle
- stationary and stationery
- dear and deer

Progress check

1 Which five methods can help you to learn spellings?

2 Which words are spelt wrongly in these sentences?

a) The farmer was carefull when puting the food in the pan latter that day.

b) The sewing was awefull and the linning so crumpled that the jacket was quiet runied.

c) He did not no weather to meet his friends or not.

3 Identify the words that are spelt wrongly:

- Wetest
- Scisors
- Potatos
- Harmful
- Recieve
- Countries
- Cieling
- Neighbour
- Flyes
- Beautyful
- Seize
- Bosses

PUNCTUATION 1

Capital letters A B

Capital letters should be used to start **proper nouns**, which include:

- people and titles

- places

- days of the week, months, holidays, special days

- countries, nations, languages, religions

- titles of books, plays, poems and films (first and main words only)

Capital letters should **always be used**:

- to start the first word of a new sentence

- when referring to yourself, as in: 'I didn't know whether I was coming or going'.

Capitals should **not be used** for:

- the seasons of the year: spring, summer, autumn, winter

- words with a national connection that has now become meaningless: brussels sprouts, french windows, venetian blinds

- some school subjects like biology, geography, maths and science, but use capitals for languages: English, French and Spanish.

Sometimes not using a capital letter can give a very different meaning. For example:

1. 'Yesterday a sixteen-year-old schoolgirl was **suspended by her head** for refusing to remove her earrings.'

2. 'Yesterday a sixteen-year-old schoolgirl was **suspended by her Head** for refusing to remove her earrings.'

Full stops

Full stops and capital letters are closely linked because the capital at the start of a sentence signals that a full stop will be needed at the end. Each completed sentence that is a statement requires a full stop at the end.

Another use of the full stop is to mark an abbreviation, i.e. to indicate where a word has been shortened, as in:

E.M.Forster	Edward Morgan Forster
etc.	etcetera
M.A.	Master of Arts

A common mistake is to string together completed statements with commas instead of full stops. Be sure to avoid this.

How to use correct punctuation to help make your meaning clear to your reader.

Commas

Commas are used to separate parts of a sentence, which helps us to understand it better. Some specific uses are to:

- separate parts of a sentence
- separate explanations
- separate items in a list
- indicate a brief pause in the sentence
- separate off names of people spoken to
- separate words such as yes, no, thank you

Always use a comma in a sentence that contains two complete statements joined by the conjunctions **however**, **nor** or **for**. When the statements are joined by **but**, **and** or **or** the comma is optional.

Question marks

Most students are clear about where to use question marks: at the end of every sentence that asks a question. Two points to remember about question marks are:

- do not write a full stop and a question mark together
- do not use a question mark in a sentence that is an **indirect** question

> **Have you finished with the cheese?**
> Direct question = use question mark
>
> **She asked me if I had finished with the cheese.**
> Indirect question = no question mark

Exclamation marks

There are three particular instances that take exclamation marks:

1. **emphatic commands**, such as: 'Stop talking at once!'
2. **vehement or strongly-felt** sentiments, such as: 'That's outrageous!'
3. **brief expressions of strong feeling**, such as: 'Help!' 'Ouch!' or 'Hooray!'

Three points to remember about exclamation marks are:

1. do not write a full stop and an exclamation mark together
2. use exclamation marks sparingly: they lose their effectiveness if you overuse them
3. **never** use more that one exclamation mark in a row

10 MINS

Inverted commas (speech marks or quotation marks)

These have three main purposes:

- to indicate **direct speech**
- to indicate the use of a **direct quotation**
- to indicate the titles of **articles** and **poems**

Speech punctuation

Direct speech is writing down what somebody said, using the exact words that they used. Here are some simple rules to follow when using speech marks (or inverted commas):

- speech marks enclose **everything** that is actually said
- the first speech mark goes at the **beginning** of the first words spoken
- the second speech marks goes **after the punctuation** at the ends of the words spoken

> **Example**
>
> The man said, 'It is not very windy today.'

When more than one person is speaking, you should start a new line every time each person begins a new speech.

> **Example**
>
> 'Hi,' said Jane.
> 'Hello,' replied Lucy. 'Have you been waiting long?'
> 'No, just a few minutes.'

Quotation

Use inverted commas around quotations.

> **Example**
>
> When Juliet is standing on her balcony, she cries out, 'O Romeo, Romeo! wherefore art thou Romeo?'

The apostrophe

In written English, apostrophes are used for one of two purposes:

1. they can be used for shortening words: **contractions**
2. they can be used to indicate **possession**

Contractions

An apostrophe is used to show that a word has been contracted (one or more letters have been missed out).

> **Example**
>
> I can't do this work. (I cannot do this work.)

The possessive apostrophe

This use of an apostrophe shows that someone owns something. It is often misused, so stick to the following rules and you won't go wrong.

1 If only one person owns something, use **'s**:

The boy's skateboard was quite new. (One boy)

2 If more than one person owns the same thing, the apostrophe comes after the **s**:

The boys' house stood in its own grounds. (More than one boy)

3 If two or more named people are in possession of something, **'s** is only added to the last name:

John, Rachael and Anthony's new school suited them very well.

4 On words with special plurals, add **'s**, not **s'** after the plural:

The men's changing room was flooded.

The children's swimming lesson was cancelled.

5 **Do not** use the apostrophe for possessives pronouns: its, his, hers, yours, theirs and our.

Progress check

Punctuate the following sentences using the appropriate punctuation marks.

1 If you haven't brought the right ingredients said the cookery teacher then you will not be cooking today

2 Why don't you come for a drink after work asked Jane later we can share a taxi home

3 I can see what you mean said Max but I do not agree with you

4 Can you come to supper asked Helen next Thursday evening

5 Were going to Beths party where therell be some live music

6 The womens course was a great success but unfortunately the mens equivalent didnt attract sufficient students

7 Alans homework was excellent but unfortunately his sisters didnt finish theirs and so their teachers werent very pleased

10 MINS

Each of the words we use in writing performs a particular function and we need to know and understand how these words all work together to enable us to write grammatically and clearly.

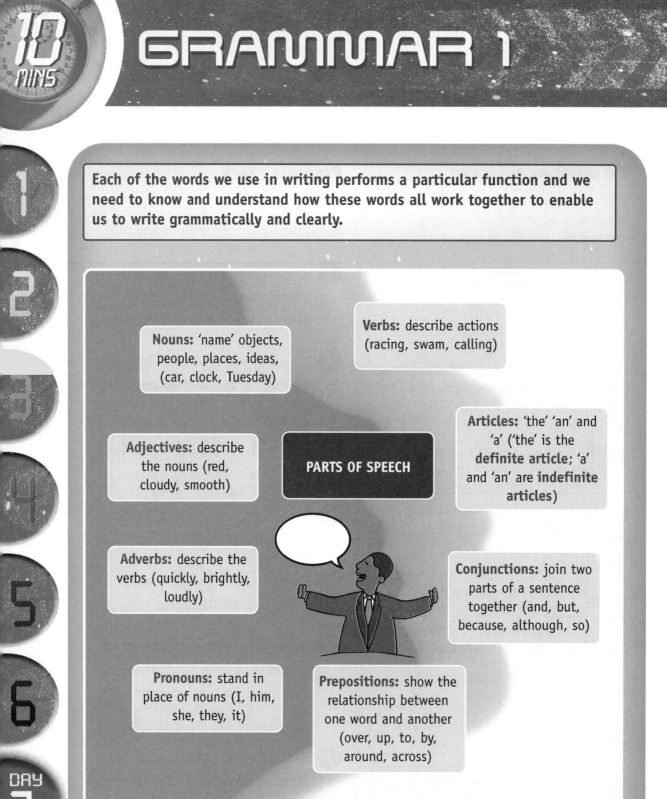

Nouns: 'name' objects, people, places, ideas, (car, clock, Tuesday)

Verbs: describe actions (racing, swam, calling)

Adjectives: describe the nouns (red, cloudy, smooth)

PARTS OF SPEECH

Articles: 'the' 'an' and 'a' ('the' is the **definite article**; 'a' and 'an' are **indefinite articles**)

Adverbs: describe the verbs (quickly, brightly, loudly)

Conjunctions: join two parts of a sentence together (and, but, because, although, so)

Pronouns: stand in place of nouns (I, him, she, they, it)

Prepositions: show the relationship between one word and another (over, up, to, by, around, across)

Sentences

One of the most basic but important things that examiners will be looking for in your work will be your ability to write in sentences. A sentence can be very short and simple or long and complicated, but all sentences follow basic rules of grammar.

> A sentence is a group of words that:
> - makes complete sense
> - has a subject
> - has its own main verb
> - usually has an object
> - starts with a capital letter
> - ends with a full stop

Types of sentence

- A **statement** tells you something.
- A **command** instructs or orders you to do something; this is called an imperative.
- A **question** asks something.
- An **exclamation** expresses strong feeling.

All sentences have a **subject** and a **verb**, and many also have an **object**. For example:

Cassie threw her teddy bear out of her cot.

The verb in this sentence is **threw**, which describes the action. The subject can be determined by asking 'Who threw?', i.e. **Cassie**. The object can be determined by asking 'What was thrown?', i.e. **the teddy bear**.

The subject and verb of a sentence should agree. For example:

The guinea pigs are always hungry.

The subject of the sentence, **guinea pigs**, is plural and, therefore, the verb of the sentence must be in the plural form too: **are** rather than **is**. If there were only one guinea pig, the singular form would be used:

The guinea pig is always hungry.

Students sometimes confuse this verb/subject agreement by writing things like 'we was' and 'I were'. Make sure that the subject and the verb agree in your writing.

Parts of speech

There are **ten** different parts of speech.
Here you can see them operating in a sentence:

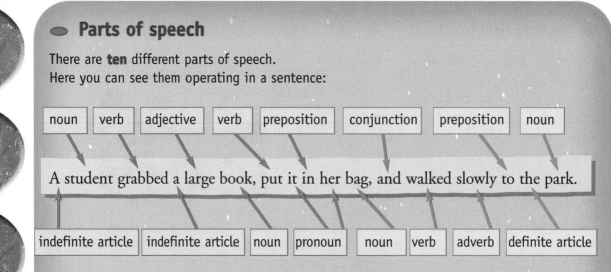

noun | verb | adjective | verb | preposition | conjunction | preposition | noun

A student grabbed a large book, put it in her bag, and walked slowly to the park.

indefinite article | indefinite article | noun | pronoun | noun | verb | adverb | definite article

Nouns

Nouns are one of the most important parts of speech. Nouns name things. They can be divided into several types:

- **common nouns:** everyday things that you can touch, smell, hear and feel (table, flower, sky, house, school)
- **proper nouns:** names given to specific people, places or things (Rachel, France, December, Birmingham, Monday)
- **collective nouns:** names given to groups of things (herd, army, flock, cluster, crowd)
- **abstract nouns:** abstract ideas (hope, religion, thought)

Interjections

These are exclamations or asides.

Pronouns

Pronouns are closely linked to nouns because they are the words used instead of a noun (she, him, it, they or her).

Adjectives

Adjectives are words that describe nouns, like the **gloomy** sky, the **yellow** car or the **burning** heat. Using adjectives in your writing can make your description more effective. Be careful not to overuse them though or your writing can sound forced and contrived.

Verbs

Verbs are another very important part of speech: they describe actions that take place, and a sentence cannot be complete unless it has a verb. Verbs also give an indication of time through the use of tenses.

DAY 7

The three basic tenses are:

● past   ● present   ● future

Students sometimes go wrong because they muddle up the tenses in their writing. For example:

We **went** to the fair in the evening and I **get** on a ride and **spilled** my drink.

Get is present tense but the other verbs are in the past tense so it should be **got**.

Adverbs

These are words that tell us more about the verb, often when, how or where something happened, for example **yesterday**, **before**, **always**, **fast**, and **everywhere**. Using adverbs can help to make your writing more descriptive and informative.

Prepositions

These are words that show the relationship between one word and another, often between a verb and a noun. For example: I ran **down** the hill; she walked **beside** the river.

Conjunctions

Conjunctions are words that join parts of sentences together, for example **and**, **but**, **or**, **because** and **so**.

Articles

Articles are a special class of three words only: the definite article is **the**, and the indefinite articles are **a** and **an**.

Progress check

1 What parts of speech are highlighted in this sentence:
Sandra **went** to the garage **because her** tyre was flat.

2 _____describe nouns, and _____ tell you more about the verb.

3 Why would you use a conjunction?

4 What parts of speech are highlighted in this sentence?
The **student** looked **in** his bag, **on** the desk and **under** his chair for **his** pen.

5 What is the difference between a proper noun and a collective noun?

6 What parts of speech are highlighted in this sentence?
The dog jumped in **the** water after **a** stick but came out with **an** old boot.

ANSWERS

Analysing arguments

1 A statement which is true.
2 A statement which expresses a point of view.
3 Appeal to the emotions.
4 'Have we had enough of this leadership?' and 'Do the people of this country want to carry on with this?' are rhetorical questions.

Writing to argue

1 To reinforce the point.
2 Newspapers, magazines, pamphlets,
3 Fact.
4 Opinion.

Persuasive writing

1 To emphasise points.
2 Relates to reader.
3 Audience, purpose.
4 Appeals to emotions.
5 Capture reader's attention.
6 Persuasive.

Writing to analyse

1 Magazine articles, extracts from books, newspaper articles, information from a website, information leaflets, advertisements.
2 The objective it is designed to achieve.
3 The readership that it is aimed at.
4 Content, language, effect.
5 Examples, comments.
6 Imagery, similes, metaphors.
7 Words, phrases.

Writing to review

1 Gives an opinion or assessment of something, e.g. a book, play, film etc.
2 Audience, purpose.
3 Fact, opinion.
4 Book, film, TV, play, music.
5 Language, effects.
6 Read reviews, write a review, read material and review it.

Writing to comment

1 a) ideas b) language use c) your own findings.
2 Newspaper.
3 Writing to analyse and review.
4 Relevant, balanced.
5 Express a view or an idea on an issue. Give an overview of issues. Give balanced or biased comment.

Writing to describe

1 To give the reader a vivid impression of the thing you are describing.
2 The opening, the use of language, the ending.
3 Capture the reader's attention.
4 Touch, taste, hearing, smell, sight.
5 Draw on your own experiences. Use literary techniques. Appeal to the senses.
6 Experiences, people, situations, conversations.

Writing about non-fiction texts

1 A newspaper report, an autobiography, an information leaflet.
2 Inform, describe, persuade, entertain, advise, explore, comment, analyse.
3 Purpose and audience.
4 a) Inform
   b) Describe/Entertain
   c) Persuade
   d) Inform
   e) Explain

Media texts

1 An advertisement, a television programme, a magazine article, a newspaper report.
2 To communicate ideas.
3 Language that appeals to the emotions.
4 Layout and presentation, content, language, organisation.

Camera work

1 A frame.
2 Moving from one shot to another.
3 To show detail, e.g. facial expression.
4 Setting.
5 Panning.
6 To give variety to the shots.

Reading Shakespeare

1 Plot is the storyline, structure is the order in which things happen.
2 Say, do, say about.
3 Point, evidence, quotation.
4 Antithesis.
5 Simile.
6 Metaphor.

Reading novels

1 Who the narrator is, which characters are introduced, what the setting is, what you notice about language and style.
2 Language, present.
3 What they say, how they behave, physical description, what they think, what others say about them.
4 The ideas that the writer explores.
5 Conflict or contrast between characters.

Reading short stories

1 First person narrative. Launches straight into the story. Arouses reader's curiosity. Short and to-the-point sentence structure.
2 The order in which events happen.
3 Who is telling the story.
4 What they say. What they do. What others say about them.
5 To give the story impact.

Reading poetry

1 Content.
2 Speaker.
3 Narrative, sonnet, elegy, ballad.
4 To make the description more vivid.
5 What, how, language, why.

Aural imagery

1 Figurative language.
2 Compares, like, as.
3 Describing an animal or an object as if they were human.
4 Alliteration.
5 Onomatopoeia.
6 Emphasise certain words. Draws lines together. Links ideas and images. Creates a musical quality.

Poems from other cultures

1 Give a sense of voice.
2 Language, attitudes, people, places, politics, beliefs, living conditions, weather.
3 Religious beliefs.
4 Shows a person caught between two cultures.
5 The value of water in an arid environment.

Comparing poems

1 Integrated.
2 Content, structure/effect, language, tone/atmosphere.
3 A comparison of the content or subject matter of each poem.
4 Structure.
5 In comparison ..., unlike ..., however ..., similarly ..., on the other hand ..., in the same way ..., in contrast to ...
6 Write about each poem separately.

Spelling

1 Look, cover, spell, write, check.
2 a) careful, putting, later b) awful, lining, quite, ruined c) know, whether
3 Wetest-wettest, scisors-scissors, potatos-potatoes, recieve-receive, cieling-ceiling, flyes-flies, beautyful-beautiful.

Punctuation

1 "If you haven't brought the right ingredients," said the cookery teacher, "then you will not be cooking today."
2 "Why don't you come for a drink after work?" asked Jane. "Later we can share a taxi home."
3 "I can see what you mean," said Max, "but I do not agree with you."
4 "Can you come to supper," asked Helen, "next Thursday evening?"
5 We're going to Beth's party where there'll be some live music.
6 The women's course was a great success but unfortunately the men's equivalent didn't attract sufficient students.
7 Alan's homework was excellent but unfortunately his sisters didn't finish theirs and so their teachers weren't very pleased.

Grammar

1   Went – verb, because – conjunction,
    her – pronoun.
2   Adjectives, adverbs.
3   To join two parts of a sentence together.
4   Student – noun, in – preposition,
    on – preposition, under – preposition,
    his – pronoun.
5   Proper noun names a specific person,
    place or thing and a collective noun
    names a group of things.
6   The – definite articles, a/an – indefinite
    articles.